Rivers
Lakes and Wetlands

Susan
McMillan

Conserving
animals and
plants in a
changing
world

BBC BOOKS

Published by BBC Books,
a division of BBC Enterprises Limited,
Woodlands, 80 Wood Lane, London W12 0TT

First published 1992

ISBN 0 563 36167 0

Designed by Neville Graham

Printed in Great Britain by
Butler & Tanner Ltd, Frome and London

4-00

UNIVERSITY OF WOLVERHAMPTON

LIB/LEND/001

Harrison Learning Centre
Wolverhampton Campus
University of Wolverhampton
St Peter's Square
Wolverhampton WV1 1RH
Wolverhampton (01902) 322305

**This item may be recalled at any time. Keeping it after it has
been recalled or beyond the date stamped may result in a fine.**
See tariff of fines displayed at the counter.

2 1 JUN 1996		20 DEC 2000
2 2 MAY 1997	- 2 JUN 1998	2 6 MAR 2001
2 6 NOV 1997	- 8 JAN 1999	1 2 NOV 2002
2 6 JAN 1998		2 6 SEP 2008
	- 2 FEB 1999	14 /10 /10
2 FEB 1998	1 7 NOV 1999	
- 1 MAY 1998	11 DEC 2000	
	11 DEC 2000	

Contents

About this book

PLANET EARTH should really be called Planet Water – far more of its surface is covered with water than land. Every animal and plant in the world depends on fresh water and this vital liquid can be found in lakes, rivers, bogs, marshes, ponds, swamps and reservoirs.

We all know how important the rainforests are to the well-being of the Earth, but lakes, rivers and other wetlands are just as important. They provide us with fresh water and food and, like the rainforests, they are home to millions of birds, reptiles, insects and plants, from South American manatees to giant water lilies.

But, like the rainforests, these lakes, rivers and wetlands and their wildlife are vanishing and who's to blame?

Yes, you guessed it, we are! We pollute the lakes, we dam the rivers and drain the marshes. We must stop destroying these places now, as they play an absolutely vital role in the health of the planet.

This book looks at some of the world's most amazing watery places, the animals and plants that live there and the problems they face. Why are alligators invading American golf courses? Why are India's swamp tigers getting shock treatment? It also has lots of suggestions on how you can take action yourself to help prevent these wonderful wetlands and their wildlife from disappearing for ever.

A watery world

Waters of life

LAKES, RIVERS, bogs, marshes, mangrove swamps, ponds and reservoirs are essential for life on earth. We fish in them, sail on them, swim in them, and drink from them; they provide electricity and food. They are magical places.

Fresh water is just as important for wildlife. Pink river dolphins hunt in the Amazon river; five million flamingoes nest on the lakes of East Africa; and over 650 tigers live in the Sunderbans mangrove swamp in India and Bangladesh.

Millions of amazing animals and plants from the world's biggest rodent to the world's smallest plant need these wonderful wetlands to live, breed and feed. They cannot survive without them.

Top: Wetlands in their natural state are perfect places for some amazing animals. The Everglades National Park in Florida is home to roseate spoonbills, egrets, herons and a host of other animals and plants.
Above: The Amazon river is one of the longest rivers in the world, and it is the last refuge for some of the world's rare animals like this Amazon river dolphin or boto.
Above left: Water provides food for many animals. In the swamps of Indonesia the magnificent Sumatran tiger hunts deer – and even fish and crabs.
Left: The North American beaver that lives in and around rivers and lakes is a natural engineer. Some countries such as Czechoslovakia have actually imported beavers to help create wetlands.

WILDSIDE WATCH

The battle for wetlands has begun! You can take action yourself to help prevent any more destruction, and this book will show you how.
● Join a group campaigning to protect rivers, lakes and wetlands.
● Keep a watch on the wildlife in your local watery places.
● Make a new home for frogs, newts and dragonflies by building a pond.

Waters of death

BELIEVE IT OR NOT, wetlands are very much like rain-forests! Both are perhaps the most important areas on earth for wildlife and people. Both are threatened by man.

Lakes, rivers and wetlands are under attack. They are drained, polluted, invaded and dammed and the animals and plants are poisoned, hunted or made homeless.

Salmon are poisoned by pollution in American rivers; crocodiles and alligators are hunted in Brazil to make leather products; and millions of tonnes of chemicals and sewage are pumped into rivers and lakes all over the world.

WILDSIDE WATCH

Pollution, poaching and wetland destruction are big issues, but no problem is too big. We can all take action to save wildlife.

● Report polluted water to your local environmental group.

● Don't buy animal skins or souvenirs made from wetland wildlife.

● Watch what you pour down the plughole, as it may end up poisoning a nearby river. Use 'greener' cleaners and detergents.

Top: We do not always look after our valuable watery places. This marsh near San Francisco is packed full of human rubbish – it's not just horrible to look at, it's lethal for birds, mammals and humans.
Above: We pollute water with chemicals and sewage. This can be invisible to us but to the animals that live there it can mean death.
Above right: Even our leisure activities can have a terrible effect on wildlife. Freshwater birds, woodland birds and even seabirds like this common tern can suffer from discarded fishing lines.
Right: Just a small part of a batch of 30,000 caiman crocodile skins confiscated by South American police. These skins would have ended up in the fashion houses of Europe, as handbags and shoes.

The young river

ALL RIVERS can be divided into three zones, with their own distinctive animals and plants, and their own particular environmental problems.

The upper zone is where the river starts, usually as a small stream among mountains or hills. Few animals can survive life right at the top, as it's a tough place with a strong current and cold water. But it's an ideal place to live for those animals that can stand the pace. The fast-flowing water brings life-giving oxygen. The animals need clean water and lots of oxygen to survive.

Caddis, mayfly, stonefly and other insects are common in young rivers worldwide. They indicate that the river is clean and unpolluted. Some plants too are ideally suited to life in the upper zone. Water starwort and water crowfoot are good examples – they are very flexible and have long roots which allow them to bend in the current but remain firmly fixed to the river bed.

Life in the fast lane

ANIMALS HAVE DEVELOPED some neat ways to survive life in the swift young river. Some animals avoid the current altogether by crawling beneath stones or burrowing into the river bed. Trout avoid the current by sheltering just downstream of a boulder or log. Others have clever devices worthy of any military survival test.

Caddis fly larvae, for example, build their own survival bags. The larva constructs a mobile home using stones, leaves or twigs stuck together with silk. This is ideal camouflage and acts as ballast against the current.

The water penny or riffle beetle has a flat body with six grasping legs and a spiny-edged shell; wedge-shaped, it jams itself into rocky crevices. One species can even survive life in the torrential Niagara Falls.

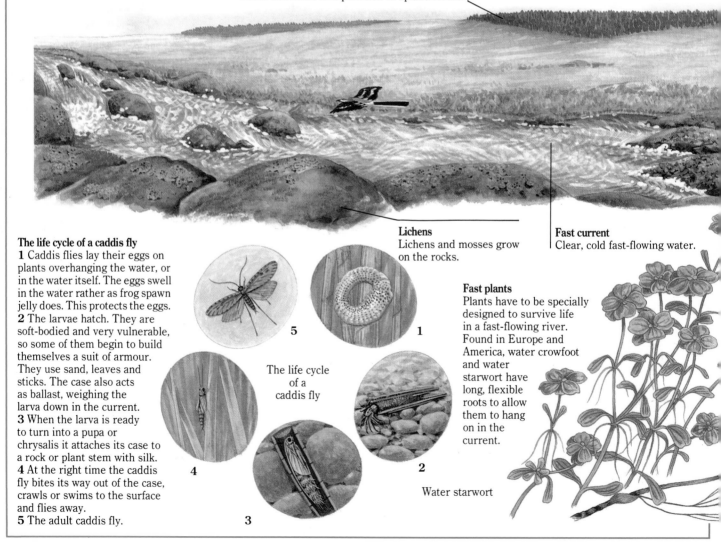

Conifer plantation
These can cause acid pollution of upland rivers.

Lichens
Lichens and mosses grow on the rocks.

Fast current
Clear, cold fast-flowing water.

Fast plants
Plants have to be specially designed to survive life in a fast-flowing river. Found in Europe and America, water crowfoot and water starwort have long, flexible roots to allow them to hang on in the current.

The life cycle of a caddis fly
1 Caddis flies lay their eggs on plants overhanging the water, or in the water itself. The eggs swell in the water rather as frog spawn jelly does. This protects the eggs.
2 The larvae hatch. They are soft-bodied and very vulnerable, so some of them begin to build themselves a suit of armour. They use sand, leaves and sticks. The case also acts as ballast, weighing the larva down in the current.
3 When the larva is ready to turn into a pupa or chrysalis it attaches its case to a rock or plant stem with silk.
4 At the right time the caddis fly bites its way out of the case, crawls or swims to the surface and flies away.
5 The adult caddis fly.

The life cycle of a caddis fly

Water starwort

The acid test

THE YOUNG RIVER is less affected by the problems of pollution that are common downstream. But, even at its source the river is threatened from acid rain.

Burning coal, gas and oil sends huge amounts of smoke and gas into the sky. These gases combine with water vapour to make acid rain clouds which can travel great distances before releasing their water as rain.

The mayflies, stoneflies, trout and other animals that depend on clean water cannot tolerate acid. They are the first to disappear. The dipper, a bird commonly found in northern rivers, relies totally on these insects for food. No food means no dippers.

But acid rain has an even more dangerous effect. It runs off the land, bringing with it aluminium and mercury from the soil. This enters the river and poisons its wildlife.

Acid rain kills aquatic life. This lake in Sweden is dead. To reduce acidity huge amounts of the chemical lime are tipped into the lake from the air. This neutralises the acid and may allow fish and other animals to live in the lake once more.

Acid rain kills trees. It damages their leaves and pine needles. This stops the trees breathing and reduces the nutrients absorbed by the trees. The acid also sinks into the soil and releases aluminium, which damages the roots so that the trees cannot absorb food or water. The solution to the problem is for industry and cars to be fitted with pollution control devices.

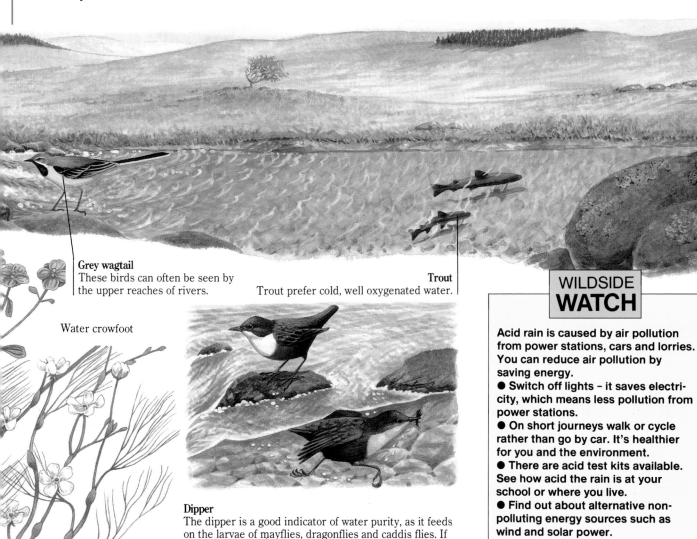

Grey wagtail
These birds can often be seen by the upper reaches of rivers.

Trout
Trout prefer cold, well oxygenated water.

Water crowfoot

Dipper
The dipper is a good indicator of water purity, as it feeds on the larvae of mayflies, dragonflies and caddis flies. If pollution kills these insects the dipper cannot survive.

WILDSIDE WATCH

Acid rain is caused by air pollution from power stations, cars and lorries. You can reduce air pollution by saving energy.
● Switch off lights – it saves electricity, which means less pollution from power stations.
● On short journeys walk or cycle rather than go by car. It's healthier for you and the environment.
● There are acid test kits available. See how acid the rain is at your school or where you live.
● Find out about alternative non-polluting energy sources such as wind and solar power.

The middle zone

THE YOUNG RIVER begins to slow down on its journey to the sea. On an undisturbed river there are many birds, fish and mammals in the middle reaches and water plants fill the shallows. The current is slower. Kingfishers nest in the banks,

salmon pass through on their way to their spawning grounds.

People have always been attracted to rivers as a source of food, water and transport. But people pollute the river, and boat traffic disturbs birds.

Slower current
The river slows down in the middle reaches. The water becomes muddier and more plants can grow.

Flowering rush
Flowering rush and other riverside plants provide cover and nest sites for birds.

Boat traffic
The wash from boats can drown the eggs and chicks of birds nesting in the reeds.

Swans
Swans breed on the middle and lower reaches of rivers, making their nests near the river banks. The wash from boats can drown the nests.

Long distance leapers

FROM THE MOMENT a salmon hatches, life is one long struggle. There are natural hazards like bears, birds and otters but that's not all. Salmon are disappearing all over the world. In 1986, on the Duwamish river in Seattle, 2500 salmon leaped suicidally from the water and died before they spawned. Pollution was blamed for this strange behaviour.

Damming rivers prevents salmon from reaching their spawning grounds and as they battle upstream, commercial and sports fishermen lie in wait. In California, the chinook salmon is now a threatened species. In Britain, the Atlantic salmon was once so common it was known as the 'poor man's fish', but overfishing means that is no longer so.

People go to amazing lengths to help salmon. Artificial waterfalls or salmon ladders are built so that the fish can bypass dams. Millions of young salmon are released into rivers and fishing is strictly controlled to protect this magnificent fish for the future.

Look before you leap! For these sockeye salmon waterfalls are not the only hazard. On their journey upstream they will also have to confront polluted water, too many fishermen and huge dams.

Trees
Willow and alder trees
are common along the
slower middle reaches
of the river. These
trees stabilise the
banks.

Water vole
Mammals like water
shrews and water
voles live here too.
Water voles have
declined in some
European countries
because of the
introduction of mink,
which prey on them.

Bulrush

Kingfisher nest holes
Kingfishers nest in muddy river banks. Riverkeepers
used to block the nest holes with stones to kill the
kingfishers. This was to prevent them eating young fish.

Angling
Fishermen can cause
problems with discarded
fishing line.

Fishing fanatics

NOT ALL FISHERMEN on the river are
human. Herons, bitterns and egrets
are all fish eaters, usually found
standing motionless in the shallows
waiting patiently to stab a passing fish.
They are threatened in two ways –
their slow flight makes them easy
targets for gunmen and high levels
of chemical pollutants have been
found in their bodies.

Kingfishers, the diving fisherbirds
of lakes and rivers, are also sensitive
to pollution. Kingfishers are found all
over the world from the Australian
kookaburra to the African pied kingfisher. They feed almost entirely on
fish, so if pollution kills their food, the
kingfishers soon disappear too.

There are more than 80 different types of kingfisher in the
world. This European kingfisher dives with remarkable
accuracy to catch fish and can make up to 100 dives per day!

The lower reaches

WHERE THE RIVER FLOWS into the sea, silt and sediment carried along by the water is deposited to form mud flats and banks, teeming with worms, shellfish and crustaceans. For migrating birds, like knot, godwit and plover, these estuary mud flats are just like airports – ideal places to stop over and refuel after a long flight.

Many of the world's great towns and cities are found around the lower reaches of rivers, together with their power stations, oil refineries and factories. This spells trouble for life in the river.

After using and polluting water, we get rid of it by flushing it away. Most of it finds its way into our rivers and estuaries.

Sewage treatment
Our waste water is cleaned at the sewage works and the 'clean' water pumped back into the river. Many sewage works are old and not designed to deal with huge amounts of sewage from growing populations.

Farm pollution
Fertilisers, liquid manure and pesticides run off farm land into the water. These chemicals cause algal blooms and kill wildlife, and can even end up in our tap water.

Chemical dumping
Pollution can be caused by the dumping of used chemicals such as car oil and detergents. These are poisonous to fish.

Fishy problems

FISHING IS A POPULAR sport throughout the world. Anglers are on the whole keen conservationists – it is in their interests to keep rivers healthy.

But there are problems. Birds get tangled up in discarded nylon fishing line, or swallow hooks or lead weights. The line gets caught around their necks and legs, the hooks stick in their throats, and swallowing lead results in blood poisoning. Any of these can cause a slow and grisly death for river birds such as swans. Most anglers are aware of all this. In many places lead weights are banned and biodegradable fishing line is available in some tackle shops.

Discarded equipment is not the only hazard for birds and animals. Fishermen have, in the past, persecuted wildlife such as ospreys, otters, cormorants and seals because they are in direct competition for the prized fish.

This mute swan family have to share their home with our rubbish.

Discarded or snagged fishing line is an invisible trap. It catches not just water birds but woodland and garden birds like this blackbird.

Factories
Factories use enormous quantities of water and after use the polluted water is often discharged directly into rivers. In most countries there are laws to control industrial pollution but this does not always stop cyanide, mercury and other poisons being pumped into the rivers of the world.

Mud flats
Estuarine mud teems with life – worms, cockles, small snails and shrimps provide food for thousands of birds such as oystercatchers, plover, knot and duck. These mud flats at the end of the river are threatened by industry, the construction of marinas, and tidal barrages.

Tidal barrages
On many of the world's rivers tidal barrages are planned or in operation. They supply power from wave energy and are a clean source of electricity. However, they affect water levels in the river and estuary, reducing the area of mud, and can therefore result in the starvation of thousands of wading birds.

Household waste
Detergents, soaps and medicines all get flushed down the plughole. These are treated in the sewage system but some dissolved chemicals still enter rivers.

Landfill sites
Rubbish is buried in landfill sites. Chemicals from old batteries and other poisonous products seep through the soil and can find their way into rivers.

WILDSIDE WATCH

Rivers need to be kept clear of pollution all the way to the sea.
● Visit a local river and see how much discarded fishing tackle you can find. Dispose of it safely.
● If you are a keen angler use non-lead weights and if possible biodegradable fishing line. It could save the lives of many swans and waterfowl.
● In Europe, groups of children are involved with Coastwatch, looking after areas of coast and estuary. If you live near an estuary set up a group of volunteer estuary watchers. Report any waste or pollution.

Nature's engineers

THE NORTH AMERICAN beaver is found in Canada and the northern United States. Its European cousin is found in small numbers in Scandinavia and Russia. Beavers can be a nuisance as they sometimes damage farmland and trees. However, they are excellent wetland engineers: their dam-building behaviour makes areas more fertile and creates wetland homes for other wildlife.

In the past beavers and also the duck-billed platypus from Australia fell victim to fur trappers, but despite this both these water-loving animals are now on the increase.

Above: A captive-bred beaver being released by Prince Bernhard of the Netherlands in the Biesbosch.
Right: This beaver has felled a small sapling. Beavers can fell over 200 trees during the construction of their dams. Foresters and farmers do not like to have beavers on their land as they damage trees and cause floods.

Reintroducing beavers to the wild

THE EUROPEAN BEAVER is not as widespread as its North American cousin. It has disappeared from many countries because of persecution by man, but now there are schemes to reintroduce them into several European countries.

The last beaver was sighted in Holland at the end of the nineteenth century. Two pairs of beavers have now been released into a wetland area on the Rhine known as Biesbosch. The Dutch are hoping that the beavers will help to increase the number of plants and enrich the soil. Children in Holland have made a contribution to the plan by raising funds and also by taking part in a beaver observation scheme.

Czechoslovakia is importing beavers too. Flown in from Norway, the beavers are being released in the hope that these expert dam builders will help conserve Czechoslovakia's dwindling wetlands. In Sweden, reintroduction schemes have been so successful that hunting has been resumed to control numbers. The Swedes have even been promoting beaver meat as a gourmet delicacy!

Mad hatters

IN THE nineteenth century the beaver was almost wiped out in the United States. They were shot and trapped to provide fur for the hat trade. An incredible 400 million beavers were killed and by 1890 only a small population remained in the mid-west. Controlling hunting and the increased use of felt to make hats saved the beavers from extinction, but in spite of this they remained absent from many areas. In the 1940s, the Federal government stepped in and began re-releasing beavers into areas where they had disappeared. They even parachuted animals into the wilderness in Idaho!

Beavers were almost wiped out to provide these very warm (and fashionable!) beaver fur hats.

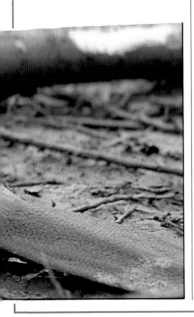

The dam-builders

Beaver dam

Dam
The beaver builds its dam to create a pond or small lake. The biggest beaver dam recorded was an amazing 700m (2300ft) long on the Jefferson river in North America, but they are usually only 20–30m (70–100ft) across.

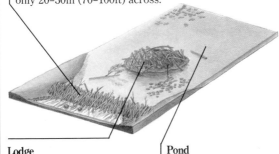

Lodge
This is a huge pile of twigs and branches where the beaver lives.

Pond
The dam forms a pond which provides a home for other wildlife.

Man-made dam

Dam
Man-made dams can range from a few metres to over 100 km (65 miles) long. The biggest dam in the world is the Itaipu Dam in Brazil.

Lake
Human dams also stop the flow of the river and form lakes, flooding the surrounding land. These man-made lakes can also provide a home for fish and other wildlife.

WE ALL KNOW that beavers build dams, but few people realise that these dams actually change the landscape, making an area ideal for other wildlife. Beavers are nature's wetland engineers.

Beaver dams create pools where fish can survive for the winter. They also slow the river down, allowing mud and silt to build up. Dammed streams have higher water levels which moisten the surrounding land, making a new wetland home for caddis flies, salmon, and muskrats. The edges are packed with plants providing food for grazing animals and moose. Biologists in America, Czechoslovakia, and Sweden have used beavers to solve man-made problems of soil erosion, overgrazing, and loss of fish.

Man-made dams are used to prevent flooding, for power and for irrigation. They cost millions of pounds. Beaver dams create a natural irrigation system that makes barren land fertile and shapes the landscape.

A strange creature

WHAT MYSTERIOUS MAMMAL has a duck-like beak and lays eggs? The platypus! They live in Australia in fast flowing rivers and, like the beaver, thousands were once killed for their fur. The fur is chestnut in colour and very soft, which made it very attractive to hunters. Up to 60 platypus pelts were used to make a single fur rug.

Today it is illegal even to own platypus fur, and the animals are now carefully protected. In some rivers fish traps are forbidden in case they catch and drown platypuses. These measures mean that, like the North American beaver, the duck-billed platypus is now on the increase.

The platypus is up to 50 cm (20 in) long and may eat up to 25,000 worms a month! They have lived virtually unchanged on Earth for 50 million years.

WILDSIDE WATCH

Although possession of platypus fur is illegal, trade in fur from many endangered animals still goes on today.
● It takes up to forty animal skins to make one fur coat or jacket. Do you think the fur looks better on humans or animals?
● Boycott shops that trade in endangered animal skins.
● You can get further information on trade in endangered species from environmental organisations (see page 62). Why not join one?

Rivers at risk

THE DAMMING of rivers is a controversial subject. Dams can be beneficial: they control the flow of the river water, provide water for irrigation, and provide cheap electricity. The reservoir that forms behind the dam can supply drinking water and an ideal location for sailing and fishing.

But what about the costs? The building of dams results in huge areas being flooded, destroying beautiful landscape, driving people from their homes and ruining wildlife habitat. Dams have caused environmental problems on the Amazon, the Nile, and on the Loire in France.

Long live the Loire!

THE RIVER LOIRE is one of France's great rivers – a thousand kilometres of unspoilt waterway famous for its chateaux and wine. The idyllic valley, its resident otters, wild boar, and rare red kites were saved early in 1990 from a flood prevention scheme which planned a series of dams at the headwaters of the Loire. Dams stop salmon migrating to their spawning ground, the changing water levels drown the nesting and resting sites for migrating birds and beautiful scenery is changed for ever.

In 1989, the bulldozers moved into the Loire valley. And so did the local people! Determined to protect their valley and its eagle owls and beavers, the people occupied the proposed site of one of the biggest dams at Serre de la Fare, stopping the destruction of their precious river. After a year-long occupation of the site the plans for the dams were shelved, but only temporarily. For the time being the wild Loire is safe. Long live the Loire!

A demonstration by the local people of the upper Loire area against plans to dam the river and the threat this would pose to the wildlife and ecology of the valley.

Red kites
These were once common in Europe. They have been persecuted and poisoned by farmers, but are still frequently seen in this natural, unspoiled area.

Grey heron
This is the grey heron, one of over 130 species of birds that live in the threatened valley.

Ombre
A rare relative of the salmon, known as the ombre, lives in the waters of the Loire.

Eagle owl
Known locally as 'le grand Duc' (the grand Duke), the European eagle owl is the biggest owl in the world.

Short-toed eagle
These birds of prey are rare in Europe but are still found in the upper Loire valley.

Where rivers run dry

SOME OF THE world's great rivers start off as raging torrents and end up as pathetic dribbles! This is the result of dam-building or when too much water is removed for agriculture, homes and industries.

In the United States, the Colorado river begins as a mighty waterway, but by the time it reaches Mexico it is reduced almost to a puddle. Most of the water is removed and diverted to Southern California. Twelve hundred dams and hundreds of kilometres of channels take water to the Californian deserts so that farmers can grow sunflowers and fruit.

In Britain and Europe, rivers are also running dry as too much water is removed for human use. How much water we waste in the future could mean life or death for river animals.

Rivers are home to birds, insects, mammals and other wildlife. If the river dries up the animals disappear. For this kingfisher a dried-up river means starvation and death.

WILDSIDE WATCH

An average family uses 500 litres (110 gallons) of water every day. The more we use the greater the chance that a river will run dry or that a valley will be flooded to make a reservoir. Being careful about using water helps to protect rivers and their wildlife.
● Don't leave the tap running when you clean your teeth. Just wet and rinse the brush.
● If you wash your family's car, use a sponge and bucket, not the hose.

Martagon lily
These rare lilies grow on the margins of the river.

Silver willow
The beautiful silver white leaves of the silver willow are a common sight along the banks of the upper Loire.

The otters' return

THERE ARE 19 species of otter in the world and five are in danger of extinction.

The European otter is one of Europe's most secretive and best loved mammals. Living in clean rivers and streams the otter has no natural predators except for man. In many parts of Europe they are now becoming extremely rare – in Holland the last otter disappeared in 1988, and they have virtually died out in Italy. There are several reasons why this has happened. The biggest culprit has been a chemical, dieldrin, used by farmers to kill insects; it also kills otters, peregrine falcons and sparrowhawks. This deadly poison has been banned in many European countries but otters are still affected in other ways by human disturbance, pollution and river bank clearance. In Eire they were still hunted as vermin until 1990.

In Britain, otters are making a comeback. They are increasing as rivers become cleaner and as people become more aware of the need to protect the natural environment. Captive-bred otters are also being released back into areas where there are suitable undisturbed, unpolluted rivers. This is a slow process but it should ensure that in these areas the otters will gradually return.

Brighter and safer water

IN BRITAIN otters are now legally protected; it is an offence to kill or injure an otter and 'otter havens' have been set up on many rivers. Organisations have been set up to conserve otters: one such is the Otter Trust in Suffolk. One of its main aims is to breed and release young otters into suitable wild areas, a process which can take many months to complete.

Young otters, usually a female and a male, are selected and kept in a large pre-release enclosure where they are disturbed as little as possible. A new 'home' on a suitable river is carefully chosen for the otters. It must have plenty of fish and no pollution. These areas are often protected as 'otter havens'. A small pen is built at the site which will be home for the otters during their first few months of freedom in their new river territory.

The otters are anaesthetised and taken to the release pen. A continuous watch is kept to check that they settle in. Food is supplied but gradually reduced so that they learn to catch food for themselves. The otters begin to venture further from the pen and soon they are behaving exactly like wild otters. To date many otters have been released into the South West and East Anglia regions of England, and some are now breeding in the wild. So, with a little assistance the future is looking brighter for the otter.

Above: A man-made otter den consisting of a box with a tunnel attached to the side. Once the captive otter is inside, the whole box is transported to the release site.
Right: The box and otter are transferred to a waiting van and driven to the selected release site on a suitable river.

Above: An otter near its home on the river bank. Pollution of rivers with pesticides has resulted in the decline of the otter in Europe. The increased use of rivers for recreation may also hasten it.

An otter with its very own 'walkman'! This radio transmitter allows scientists to track the otter to study its behaviour and distribution.

WILDSIDE WATCH

Otters are in danger all over the world. They need your help.

● Otter rivers must be protected from pollution, disturbance and overfishing. Campaign to stop river pollution – you may be helping an otter!

● Otters are shy, nocturnal animals and difficult to see. But you can look for signs such as tracks, droppings or otter holts on undisturbed rivers.

● If you are lucky enough to see an otter, contact your local conservation group. You will be helping biologists to find out more about numbers and distribution of otters.

The dirtiest river?

THE GANGES IS A HOLY RIVER sacred to the Hindu religion. It starts as a glacier 4000 m (13,000 ft) high in the Indian Himalayas and finishes 2500 km (1600 miles) away in the Sunderbans swamps.

Three hundred million people depend on the Ganges. It provides drinking water and transport; it's the laundrette and cattlewash; it's a sewer and carrier of disease and it's home to a huge array of wildlife.

Mynah birds, parrots, kites and crows live on the banks together with deer, boar, wildcats and jackals; and in the river itself live the Ganges river dolphin and the gharial or gavial, a long-snouted fish-eating crocodile.

The wildlife of the Ganges and most other great rivers is under increasing pressure from people and pollution. Together with the river Rhine, the Ganges is one of the dirtiest rivers in the world.

Trouble in the Ganges

WITH SO MANY PEOPLE relying on the river, the animals that live there are suffering some major problems.

Water is diverted to farmland; tonnes of soil are washed into the water; dams cut off sections of the river. Combined with a billion gallons of sewage per day plus industrial waste, fertilisers and pesticides, this sacred river is now an unholy mess.

Despite the pollution however, the river is still home to one of the world's rare dolphins, the susu or Ganges river dolphin. There are thought to be 5000 of these dolphins in the rivers of India and Nepal, but they are under threat. Their river home is shrinking at an alarming rate. They are cut off by dams and poisoned by chemicals. Additional hazards include entanglement in nets and harpooning. Dolphin meat and oil are used for 'medicine' and food.

A 'Clean Ganges' campaign hopes to clean up the Ganges in the next few years which is good news for both the people and wildlife of India.

Above right: These devout Hindus are bathing at Varanasi, the holiest and dirtiest city on the Ganges. They drink and bathe to wash away their sins - in water that receives industrial pollution and a billion gallons of sewage every day.
Right: The gavial or gharial can grow up to 6.5 m (22 ft) long and lives in the rivers of India. Gavials have been on Earth for over 70 million years and are now an endangered species because of hunting and destruction of their river homes.

The bodysnatchers

FOR INDIANS the sacred Ganges washes away sin and transports the dead to heaven. In one city alone the remains of 100,000 bodies are thrown into the river every year. Disease and the foul stench have driven the government to action – helped by flesh-eating turtles.

Ganges river turtles eat anything that's dead. Local people catch them for food and numbers have declined. They have now been declared a protected species and the government is helping these turtles by setting up egg-hatching programmes. The government hope that huge numbers of turtles will soon be munching their way through the floating corpses.

Ganges river turtle
The river Ganges is home for flesh-eating turtles, which eat any dead meat, including human corpses.

Dolphins in China

THERE ARE FIVE TYPES of river dolphin in the world. The boto in South America, the Indus river dolphin from Pakistan and the baiji from China are among the world's rarest aquatic mammals.

The baiji is perhaps the most endangered of them all. Like the giant panda the baiji is unique to China. Their population in the Yangtze river is only two to three hundred. Life for these graceful dolphins is extremely hazardous. An average day for a dolphin includes facing ships' propellers, fishing nets and explosions.

Reserves are being set up to protect the estimated 1000 that remain. But only rapid action will save these dolphins from extinction.

Chinese river dolphin
The Chinese river dolphins or baiji have a hard life in the busy Yangtze River. Only a few hundred still survive there.

WILDSIDE
WATCH

India is not the only country with dirty rivers. Almost every country has its own pollution problems.
● **Look out for pollution – if a local factory is polluting a river report it.**
● **You probably don't have dolphins living in your local river, but find out what does live there.**
● **Join an organisation campaigning for clean rivers where you live and in the rest of the world.**

The big clean-up

INDUSTRIAL WASTE, oil, sewage, heavy metals, plastic, dead bodies! All this rubbish finds its way into the world's rivers, accidentally or not.

Rivers have always been regarded as ideal for getting rid of human waste, but now many countries have started a big clean-up. London's River Thames has made a spectacular recovery over the last thirty years. Water birds, fish, even the pollution-sensitive salmon have returned.

In parts of Europe and the United States, laws stop pollution of rivers, but these are not always effective. Too many rivers are still pumped full of an undrinkable cocktail of pollutants and for some of the wildlife it may already be too late.

A river in danger

THE RHINE is the longest river in Europe. It flows through the industrial heartland of Germany and six other countries. On its passage to the North Sea each country adds a lethal mixture of industrial chemicals and waste. Cleaning up the Rhine is a mammoth task. In the 1970s, environmental groups and scientists from all the countries on its banks began the big clean up and fish began to return.

But in 1986, an accident at a chemical warehouse in Switzerland sent agricultural chemicals, solvents and mercury spewing into the Rhine. Millions of fish, water birds, eels and insects were killed. Further down the river, sheep drank the water and died. A 328km (205 miles) stretch of the river was declared biologically dead.

Conservationists, politicians and scientists still hope that strict international laws will control pollution. It is hoped that by 2000 the Rhine will be so clean that salmon will return.

Drinking water
In Germany villages and cities depending on the Rhine had to stop drinking water after the fire.

Mercury
200kg (440lb) of mercury settled in the mud on the river bed. Biologists fear that this mercury, which cannot be removed, will enter the food chain, poisoning fish-eating birds and people in the future.

The water is tested regularly to find out how effective pollution controls are.

Electric fish

DESPITE ALL the computer wizardry of the 1990s scientists are still finding out that nature is by far the best pollution monitor.

Biologists on the river Thames are using the elephant nose fish from West Africa to detect river pollution. These fish live in murky African rivers and use electric impulses to navigate and to communicate with each other. In polluted water they send out a fast electrical signal warning other fish. The fish are placed in Thames water and by recording the impulses the Thames biologists know if the water becomes polluted.

The strange elephant-nose fish uses its sensitive 'trunk' to detect levels of pollution.

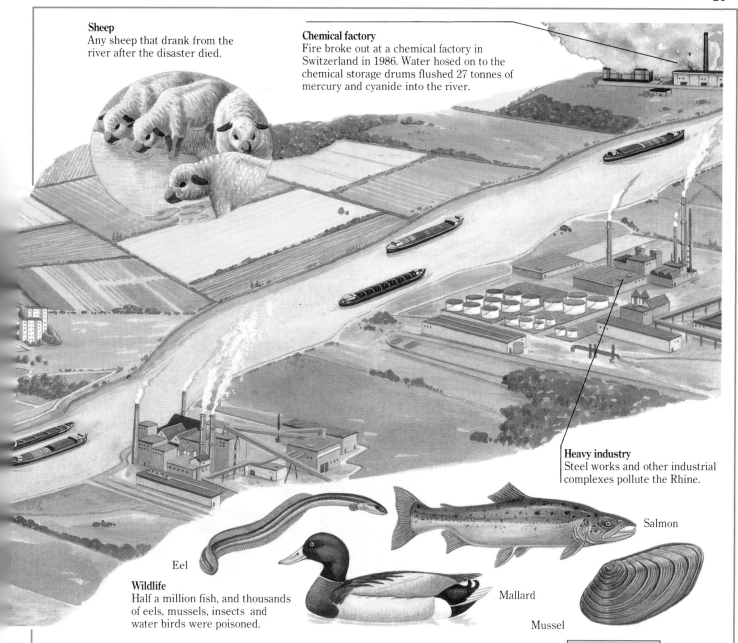

Sheep
Any sheep that drank from the river after the disaster died.

Chemical factory
Fire broke out at a chemical factory in Switzerland in 1986. Water hosed on to the chemical storage drums flushed 27 tonnes of mercury and cyanide into the river.

Heavy industry
Steel works and other industrial complexes pollute the Rhine.

Salmon

Eel

Mallard

Mussel

Wildlife
Half a million fish, and thousands of eels, mussels, insects and water birds were poisoned.

A poisonous mix

NEARLY ALL RIVERS flow into the sea, so marine wildlife can also be affected by river pollution.

Twelve types of whale feed around the mouth of the St Lawrence river in Canada including the beluga, or white whale. But these white whales are dying. The river carries a toxic soup of waste from industries upstream which poisons the belugas' food. The bodies of these whales contain chemicals at such high levels that technically they qualify as toxic waste. The river is being cleaned up but for the belugas it is probably too late. Only a few hundred remain in the St Lawrence.

Beluga or white whales are found around coasts and estuaries in Canada and the Arctic. They were once hunted for food and for their oil, which was used in soap and margarine. Today they are under threat from pollution. The total population of beluga whales is estimated at 40–55,000.

WILDSIDE WATCH

If you live near a stream or river you can help to keep it clean and healthy.
● Rivers are often convenient dumps for rubbish. Get together with a local conservation group and clean up a local river.
● Avoid chemical lavatory cleaners which hang in the cistern or basin. They may make your loo flush blue, but most of them contain a nasty chemical called paradichlorobenzene which pollutes water.
● Keep a watch for polluted stretches of river, and report any that you see to your local environmental health officer.

Upsetting the balance

WHEN PEOPLE THINK of nature conservation they always think of parrots and pandas. It's unlikely that people will think of piranhas, pigtoe mussels and crayfish! But they are just as important as the largest or cuddliest mammal.

We must conserve all animals as even the smallest fish is necessary to the natural balance of a river. The activities of people upset this natural balance not only with pollution, but also by introducing alien species like coypu and crayfish.

Too many coypu

PEOPLE UPSET the balance of nature by introducing alien species. Originally from South America the coypu or nutria has been introduced into the United States and Europe. They are found in rivers and wetlands, where they feed on roots and water plants.

Their soft fur was highly prized and fur farms were set up across the world. Many escaped and numbers began to grow . . . and grow! In Louisiana, 20 coypu were brought in for fur farming, but by the 1950s there were thought to be 20 million living wild in the state. In Europe the coypu can be a pest: its burrows damage farm land and destroy the banks of rivers.

The velvety brown fur of the coypu is perfect for waterproofing and warmth and was also very attractive to fur farmers.

Piranhas can be vegetarian!

THE MOST ferocious freshwater fish in the world is the piranha fish which lives in slow moving rivers in South America. Only four out of the 16 types of piranha are dangerous to man and attacks are rare although a shoal of 1000 of these 'river sharks' can attack and reduce a large dog to a skeleton in less than a minute!

Alligators, crocodiles, river dolphins and giant otters feed on piranhas, and in some areas of South America there are fears that the decline in these animals will result in an increase of piranhas.

But not all of them are bloodthirsty carnivores: in the Amazon river there are vegetarian piranhas too, which are vital to the rainforest. The piranhas eat fruit that falls into the river. They then drop the seeds further up or down the river where they grow into trees. So even small ugly fish are important!

This vegetarian piranha is vital to the Amazon rainforest, as it helps to transport seeds up and down the river, allowing new trees to grow.

Killer crays!

CRAYFISH are freshwater crustaceans which live in rivers, lakes and streams. They are popular food for otters, mink and people. Across Europe these freshwater 'lobsters' have been dying from a killer fungus introduced by the American signal crayfish, an alien species reared on crayfish farms.

In Britain, many foreign crayfish have escaped from fish farms into rivers. European, Turkish and Louisiana red swamp as well as American signal crayfish are invading British waters, carrying plague. There are fears that the native white-clawed crayfish could be wiped out.

The American signal crayfish is wiping out Europe's native crayfish. It breeds rapidly, is very strong and carries a fungus plague that attacks the shell of native European crayfish.

Muskrats v. mussels

THE MUSKRAT occurs all over the United States and Canada, in marshes, lakes, ponds and rivers. Perfectly adapted for swimming, with webbed feet and a rudder-like tail, it spends much of its time in the water where it feeds on cat-tails and waterlilies with some crayfish, mussels and small fish thrown in.

On the Tennessee river the shiny pigtoe mussel is a favourite muskrat meal. They are now an endangered species because of pollution and industry along the river. It is now being cleaned up but the mussels cannot recover because the muskrats are munching their way through them. Hunting is being proposed to stop them from exterminating the mussels.

The muskrat has been deliberately introduced to Europe for fur and it can now be found from France to Siberia. Their burrowing habits have caused problems particularly in the Netherlands where they frequently damage dykes and dams.

Above: Muskrats are mainly vegetarian but some take crayfish, crabs and mussels. They are excellent swimmers - they can swim up to 100 m (330 yds) under water and stay submerged for 17 minutes.

WILDSIDE WATCH

All animals need our protection. Scientists estimate that the world is losing one species every day!
● Support campaigns to protect insects, fish, and small creatures – they are just as important as tigers and gorillas.
● See if there are any objects in your house that come from an endangered species. You may not find ivory but what about coral or tortoiseshell?
● Don't buy souvenirs or ornaments made from animals.

A lakeside sanctuary

NORTH AMERICA, East Africa, the English Lake District and Scandinavia are all famous lakelands. Lakes are excellent places for wildlife watching. In northern lakes large mammals like moose and deer drop by for a drink; bats feed on the insects that dance on the water's surface and ducks and grebes nest on the banks. Muskrats, mink and terrapins all make their homes in or around these lakeside sanctuaries.

A watery haven

IN THE SHALLOW water at the edge of a typical northern lake, reeds and other plants grow. These plants are great hiding places for green frogs, painted turtles, muskrats and moorhens.

Plankton, small insects and fish such as pike and yellow perch live in the open water where there is plenty of sunlight. In the deeper waters live animals such as carp, catfish and bloodworms, that can cope with the darkness, cold and lack of oxygen.

All the animals and plants of the lake are linked in a food web. Sunlight allows algae to grow, plankton eat the algae. Perch and char eat the plankton, and pike and zander eat these smaller fish; otters, herons and muskrats eat all sorts of fish. If overfishing or pollution removes a link in the food web every animal in the lake is affected.

Painted turtle
These small reptiles are not really turtles, but terrapins which feed on lake plants.

Green frog
Ponds are not the only homes for frogs. The green frog is a common amphibian in the shallow waters of North American lakes.

Diving beetle
These large beetles are commonly found in ponds and lakes. They dive under water to hunt for food using a bubble of air like a sub-aqua diver's air tank.

Cranes in China

UNTIL RECENTLY the Siberian crane was thought to be on the verge of extinction in Asia. Only 200 were thought to remain in the world, but in 1981 about 100 of these graceful birds were found alive and well on Poyang lake in China. The lake is a nature reserve, and to protect the cranes hunting, drainage and pollution are now strictly controlled. Other flocks have been discovered in China and the USSR, so the future is looking brighter for these great white cranes.

The birds have an elaborate courtship display. Males and females dance with each other, prancing, leaping, and bowing – the breakdancers of the bird world!

The Siberian crane migrates from Russia to India and China. It was once thought to be on the verge of extinction and even now is still an endangered bird.

Red-breasted merganser
Red-breasted mergansers and grebes feed on the fish, eels, and insects in the lakes.

Muskrat
Reeds at a lake's edge often house muskrats. The reeds are one of its favourite foods in lakeside areas.

Pike
Pike are carnivorous fish and are at the top of the lake food chain.

Yellow perch
Perch are common fish in northern lakes. They live in the top 50m (170ft) of water but breed in the shallows. The yellow perch is a North American species almost identical to the European variety. Perch have been introduced into Australian lakes.

Menacing mink

THE NORTH AMERICAN mink is found naturally in Canada and the United States. They were introduced to Europe to provide fur, but soon escaped from the fur farms and set up home on the waterways of Britain, Scandinavia, Iceland and Russia.

In Britain, they were soon 'Wanted Dead or Alive' by farmers, gamekeepers and conservationists as they munched through trout and young game birds. Watervoles are a favourite mink snack too as are moorhen, coot, mallard and seabirds. They were even thought to drive otters away from rivers.

However, some scientists believe that the idea of the 'killer mink' is a myth. They do not compete with otters for food or space, and the decline of fish and birds may be due to man. They are still hunted and trapped but perhaps their reputation is undeserved.

The North American mink is a killer! Or is it? Mink are powerful swimmers and have invaded the lakes and rivers of Europe, but they may not be the killers of other wildlife that we thought.

Bats beware!

MANY BATS feed near water where gnats and flies hang out every evening. In South America, some bats even catch fish and frogs.

In Europe, the Daubenton's bat often hunts low over the surface of lakes and ponds. Also known as the 'water bat' it is still common in Britain, but rare in Germany and Austria. Anglers occasionally catch them by accident but the main threat is from loss of old trees in which they roost.

The rare pond bat is endangered throughout Europe too because of loss of ponds and chemical pollution as well as destruction of roosting sites.

The Daubenton's bat or water bat hunts near lakes and ponds. It is threatened by pollution and loss of roosting trees.

WILDSIDE WATCH

We need to protect lakes from pollution and disturbance to wildlife.
● **Visit a lake and find out what animals and plants live there. Watch for problems caused by pollution or people.**
● **All bats need protecting. You can help by putting up a bat box. Conservation organisations or your local library should have information on how to make one.**
● **Mink were introduced into many countries for fur. If you disagree with the fur trade persuade your family not to buy fur products.**

Vital water plants

ALGAE, MOSSES, WATERLILIES, reeds, grasses and trees – hundreds of plants can be found in or beside water, ranging in size from the microscopic to the gigantic.

These green plants are vital. They provide the food on which all water life depends. Their stems, leaves and roots also provide protection and nest sites for wildlife. Insects hang on to them, birds walk on them and fish eat them. Humans eat them too – in Mexico, the local people collect the protein-packed algae from lakes and make biscuits.

Plants can also talk to us. Too much algae tells us that a lake may be polluted by sewage or farm fertilisers. Without the vital water plants fresh water would be devoid of life.

Smallest algae, largest lilies

ALGAE ARE MICROSCOPIC plants. Small quantities of algae are essential for freshwater life, as food for insects and fish, but algae multiply explosively if fertilising chemicals like phosphate and nitrates pollute the water. These chemicals are plant foods. Sewage and farm pollution mean that the algae get an overdose of plant food causing an algal bloom which turns the water into a thick green soup. The algae use up the oxygen in the water, suffocating and poisoning fish. The Great Lakes in North America and Europe's reservoirs have suffered from algal blooms affecting drinking supplies as well as the wildlife.

Algae are the smallest water plants and the giant Victoria water lily of South America is the largest. The leaves of the lily are over 2 m (7 ft) across, covered on the underside with air-filled floats. These floating giants offer a home to beetles, ants and lizards. They are so big that they can even support the weight of a child.

Plants are vital to the Amazon river food chain. Floating meadows of water plants provide food for millions of insects. Scientists have counted up to 700,000 in 3 square metres (33 square feet) of meadow! The insects in turn are food for fish and birds.

Right: Giant Amazon water lily leaves are so big and strong that you could probably sit on one – without sinking! Inset: Algal cells like these may look harmless and very pretty under the microscope, but pollution causes them to explode in numbers. These algal blooms are poisonous to wildlife and to us.

Beetles to the rescue

LAKE MOONDARRA is a freshwater lake in Australia. A floating fern from Brazil was accidentally introduced to the lake and by the 1970s this fast-growing water plant had taken over. Scientists estimated that 50,000 tonnes of the fern were suffocating the lake, so there was little room, or oxygen, for any other life.

The problem was solved, not by a chemical herbicide, but by a beetle which eats the fern in its native Brazil. Australian scientists introduced the beetle to Lake Moondarra and within a year these hungry vegetarian insects had munched their way through the lot.

The waters of Lake Moondarra were choked with ferns (left). Two years later the beetles had done their work (right) and the surface is now clear.

Water plants for space?

WATER HYACINTHS are pretty floating plants. They are found all over the world where they quickly spread over lakes, rivers and swamps. But these plants can be very useful in cleaning up sewage. They remove harmful chemicals, leaving safe water behind. Scientists think they may be useful to future space missions, when astronauts will be able to dispose of their sewage and recycle water by using these plants.

Water hyacinths block out sunlight from the water so it quickly becomes stagnant and kills other wildlife.

WILDSIDE WATCH

The balance between algae, other plants and animals needs to be maintained.
● Look out for algae in lakes and ponds and report it.
● Never swim in water which is suffering from an algal bloom.
● Plants are essential for wildlife for nest sites, protection and food. If you have a pond make sure it is well stocked with plants.

Pests and pollution

WATER IS ESSENTIAL for survival. It is a giver of life – and death. Pollution is not the only danger in the water: parasitic diseases like malaria, which affects 300 million people every year, yellow fever and sleeping sickness are transmitted by insects that rely on water to breed.

Only a small percentage of water animals are dangerous like the mosquito: on the contrary, most small animals and insects that live in rivers, lakes and wetlands are extremely useful. They tell us how clean or polluted the water is.

Waterwatch

HOW HEALTHY is the water in your local river or pond? It's easy to check up on the health of the water by looking at it: if it's smelly and dirty it may be polluted. By becoming a pollution detective you can give the water a more detailed health check through looking at the animals and plants that live there. Some water animals can live quite happily in polluted water while others must have clean water to survive.

If you cannot find any animals at all the waterway may be dead, killed by pollution – and all good detectives should find out whodunnit.

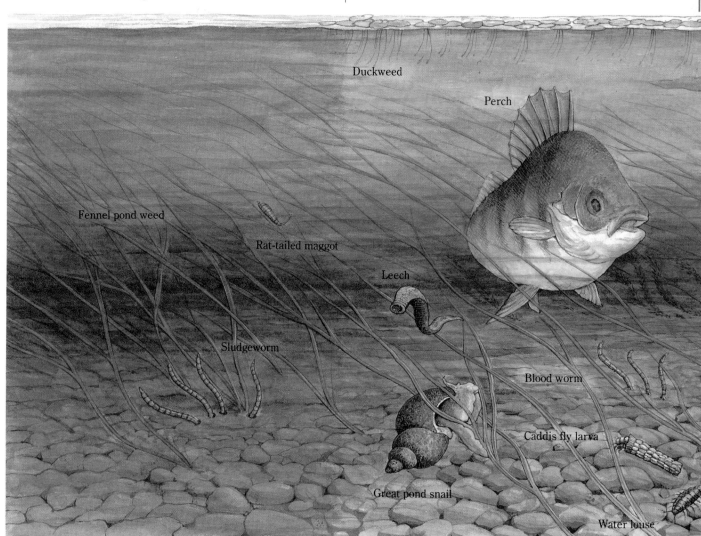

Heavily polluted water
The creatures that live happily here are those that can tolerate the low oxygen levels in polluted water. If you find only these creatures during your pond or river dipping they will tell you that the water is heavily polluted.

Moderately polluted water
Where there is not quite so much pollution and therefore still a reasonable amount of oxygen more animals can survive. If you find the following creatures but no dragonfly larvae, mayfly larvae or freshwater shrimps the water is moderately polluted.

River and pond dipping

WHY NOT INVESTIGATE what's living in water near you? All good water detectives have a basic kit consisting of a long-handled net, a kitchen sieve, some plastic containers and a magnifying glass. Sweep the net through the water and then tip any contents into a container. If you examine this closely you should find some water animals and get an idea of how clean the water is. Keep on dipping, and record what you find. Put the animals back when you have finished your investigation.

Water lily

Freshwater shrimp

Young trout

Mayfly larva

Freshwater mussel

Stonefly larva

Clean water
Some creatures can only live in clean, well oxygenated water where there is no pollution. Their presence indicates that the water is clean and unpolluted.

Mosquitoes spell danger

WHAT'S THE MOST dangerous animal in the world? The tiger? The cobra? Believe it or not, it's the tiny mosquito. Mosquitoes are found from the tropics to the Arctic. Although many are harmless to humans others suck blood and transmit the parasite that causes malaria. A million people die from malaria every year.

Such a dangerous animal has to be controlled. Mosquitoes lay their eggs in water, so swamps and marshes are drained or sprayed with pesticides to kill the mosquitoes' eggs and larvae. This destroys the homes of other wildlife and pollutes the water, but it has little effect on the mosquitoes. They become resistant to the pesticides and find other areas to breed. An anti-malarial vaccine would be a better answer to the problem.

The dreaded mosquito! These insects can transmit malaria, dengue fever and yellow fever. They are extremely dangerous.

WILDSIDE WATCH

Many organisations are helping people in Africa and Asia suffering from waterborne diseases like malaria, bilharzia and river blindness. They need your support.
● Organise a sponsored event or bazaar at your school, to raise money for charities working in developing countries.
● Keep your own pollution watch – test the water in your local pond, river or lake.
● Water can be dangerous, not just from pollution and insects. Always take care near rivers and lakes.

Frogs and toads

SCIENTISTS are hopping mad. Recent surveys have shown that all over the world frogs, toads and salamanders are disappearing at an alarming rate. The cause of this decline is rather a mystery. It could be the destruction of ponds, the use of pesticides or acid rain. Their disappearance could even be caused by global warming. Luckily, amphibians have friends. In many countries enthusiastic frog fanatics are banding together to save them from extinction.

Amphibians in danger

THE BEAUTIFUL golden toad is only found in a small area of forest in Costa Rica. Thousands were collected for sale as exotic pets, but although trade has now been banned they are still declining. Boreal toads and tiger salamanders in the United States and natterjack toads in Europe are facing the same fate.

So what's the cause? In the Colorado Rockies acid rain is stored in ice and snow over winter. When it melts in spring acid is released into the lakes just as tiger salamanders'

eggs are developing. The young salamanders cannot survive in acid water. Other pollutants such as pesticides are absorbed straight into the bloodstream of moist-skinned amphibians.

But pollution is only part of the problem. Amphibians' homes are being rapidly destroyed: in Britain, 182,000 ponds have been lost in the last 30 years. There may be an even more serious cause: amphibians might be disappearing because of climatic changes possibly caused by global warming.

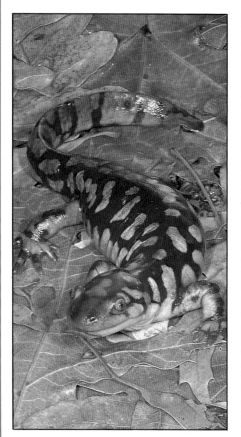

Left: The eastern tiger salamander from America is threatened by acid rain.
Above: In the Rocky Mountains of Colorado, boreal toads are mysteriously declining. They were once so common that local people reported that it was difficult not to tread on them when walking. They are now hard to find.
Right: These beautiful golden toads are only found in one small area of forest in Costa Rica, but they are now disappearing, and no-one has managed to find out why.

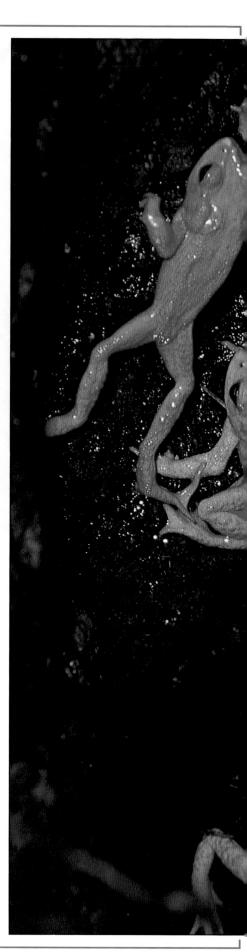

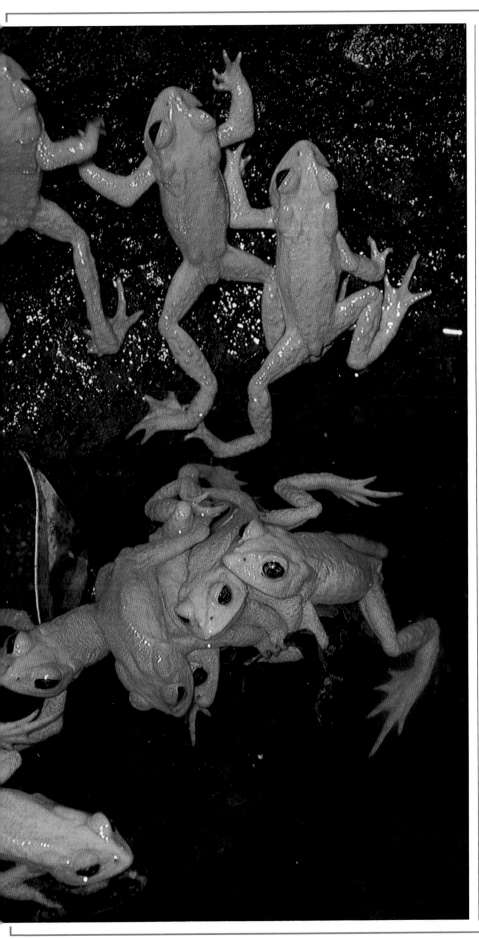

Frog patrol

IN BRITAIN, the number of freshwater homes for frogs, toads and newts has fallen by a fifth in the last 30 years. Ponds have been drained, used as rubbish dumps and built on, and many are surrounded by motorways or major roads.

Frogs and toads always return to their pond of origin to spawn. During the journey to their birthplace they may have to cross busy roads. The result? Squashed toads and flat frogs.

But never fear – frog patrols to the rescue! In Humberside, England, children from local conservation groups form road crossing patrols for frogs. These enthusiastic groups wait near busy roads during the breeding season to collect frogs which they carry safely across the road to their pond. Thousands of amphibians have hitched a ride to safety in the buckets of the frog patrollers.

These young frogs will be transported safely across a road by bucket. Frogs always return to the pond they were spawned in to breed.

WILDSIDE WATCH

Frogs and toads need protection.
● **Make a pond for a frog – even an old washing-up bowl will do. If you're lucky you may get frogs and toads breeding there.**
● **It's great fun collecting frogspawn, but try to return the young frogs to the pond.**
● **If you decide to keep exotic frogs and toads as pets make sure they have been bred in this country.**

Farming the waters

PEOPLE ENJOY RIVERS, lakes and wetlands for days out, fishing, birdwatching and sport. But water is also used to supply food, such as fish, rice and even frogs' legs.

Throughout the world water is farmed for food. Scotland's lochs are farmed for salmon and trout, which are reared in underwater cages. Some lake and marshland reserves, such as India's Keoladeo National Park, were originally preserved so that hunters could 'farm' waterfowl that breed there. In Asia man-made wetlands are specially created to farm rice – and frogs.

A maharajah's duck farm

ONE OF THE finest waterfowl reserves in the world was once farmed for its birds. Keoladeo, a wetland area in India, was originally preserved so that the maharajahs (the princes of India) could shoot ducks for sport. Signs in Keoladeo record the numbers of birds shot by visiting officials, princes and maharajahs. In 1938, the Viceroy of India and his shooting party shot 4273 birds in a single day. Shooting has not been permitted since 1964 and the area is now a National Park. Over 300 species of bird, including 80 types of duck, now live there in safety. Although famous for its birds Keoladeo is also a sanctuary for a range of mammals, including fishing cats, porcupines, hanuman monkeys and deer.

Top: These nineteenth century duck shooters may look like a comedy duo from a silent movie but at Keoladeo such shooting parties were responsible for the deaths of up to 4500 birds per day (above).

A fishy business

IN SCOTLAND, Norway, Canada and Iceland fish farming is booming. In Scotland, salmon and trout are farmed in fresh and salt water lochs, in underwater cages where the young fish are fed, protected and kept clean. The farms have created jobs and money for local people.

But conservationists are worried about how the farms affect the lochs and the wildlife that lives and feeds there. There are many problems: the fish are treated with a chemical which kills parasites. It also kills shrimps, mussels, crabs and lobsters. Herons, otters and seals are attracted to the cages to raid the fish and they may be shot for stealing; surplus fish food

drops through the cages and can pollute the loch; farmed salmon are not native to Scotland, and if these 'aliens' escape from farms they can have a terrible effect on species native to the area (see page 22).

Fish farming has its good and bad points, which all need to be carefully considered so that Scotland's famous lochs are not damaged.

Supper time at a trout farm in a Scottish loch. The amount should be carefully monitored so that uneaten food does not end up polluting the water.

Rice and frogs' legs

IN ASIA artificial wetlands are created to grow rice. In India, a variety of frogs live in these paddy fields. They are harvested along with the rice and exported to western Europe to provide frogs' legs for gourmet dinners.

The frogs control pests in the paddy fields, as they eat the insects that eat the rice. When the frogs are removed the pests increase and the rice crops are ruined. The local people then have to use chemicals to control pests, which poison the water, the wildlife and the people. The World Wide Fund for Nature has started a project to show how important it is for the rice crop to allow the frogs to remain undisturbed.

Many animals like this Indian frog are important in controlling pests. If they are removed the pests increase.

WILDSIDE WATCH

Much of our food supply depends on water. It's not just fish, rice and duck; fruit, cereals, and many other foods cannot be produced without water.
● Pesticides can be harmful to us as well as wildlife. Try to buy organic food, grown without chemicals.
● About 1000 seals, 2000 cormorants and 200 herons are shot every year on Scottish fish farms. Find out about the case for and against fish farming.

Fish catchers

OSPREYS AND FISH EAGLES are birds of prey that have adapted to a watery life. The osprey is perfectly designed for fishing. From the lakes of China to the rivers of North America, these 'fish hawks' catch their supper with their feet. They have long talons and their toes are covered with spines which help them grasp their slippery prey. They also have excellent eyesight: they can spot a bream or carp beneath the surface from 50 m (165 ft) high.

Fish eagles are also expert fishers. The African fish eagle, the American bald eagle and the white-tailed sea eagle (recently reintroduced into Britain from Scandinavia) all live, feed and breed near water.

Ospreys v DDT

DURING THE 1960s, birds of prey all over Europe and America began to decline. The culprit? DDT, a chemical used to kill insects. Pesticides like DDT are persistent which means they stay in the environment for a very long time. It affects animals in a number of ways; it can kill them outright, it affects reproduction and it weakens them, so they are more susceptible to disease and easily caught by predators.

DDT affects plankton. Fish eat plankton and ospreys eat the fish. In America, DDT accumulated in the ospreys' bodies. They laid eggs with paper-thin shells which broke before the chicks could hatch. The effects were devastating: ospreys, eagles, hawks, and falcons came close to extinction in many countries.

In the early 1970s DDT was banned. Ospreys along with peregrine falcons and sparrowhawks began slowly to recover, but DDT can still be found in the environment.

DDT and other pesticides were responsible for the deaths of many birds of prey in the 1950s and 1960s. Today ospreys are rarely affected by pesticides but a small number die from flying into high-voltage wires.

The latest threat

IN SCOTLAND, ospreys are a big tourist attraction. Thousands of people flock to see them nesting at the Loch Garten Bird Reserve. Early this century, ospreys were hunted to extinction in Scotland by landowners who feared for their prized trout and salmon. In the 1950s an osprey pair returned to Loch Garten. They now breed successfully throughout the Highlands.

Nests have to be closely guarded by barbed wire and a 24-hour watch, to protect them from egg collectors. These people will stop at nothing to get osprey eggs for their collections, even though the pastime is illegal. In 1990, eight nests were robbed. In spite of these setbacks, the careful protection of Scottish ospreys by conservationists means that by 1990 there were 54 breeding pairs in the Highlands, a conservation success.

An osprey feeds its young. Ospreys normally lay three eggs. The young hatch within five weeks and are fed exclusively on fish – up to five fish a day. The same nest may be used for years, sticks being added every year until the nest reaches huge proportions, sometimes 3 m (10 ft) across!

A frontyard fixture

OSPREY POLES are the fashionable thing, if you live in Martha's Vineyard, an island off the coast of Massachusetts – it certainly beats having a bird table in your garden.

American ospreys were badly affected by DDT. Once it was banned the osprey had a chance to recover, but at Martha's Vineyard life still wasn't easy. The building of more holiday homes there meant that many old trees had been felled. No trees mean no nesting sites and by 1971, only four ospreys remained.

To tempt the birds back the local people began putting up osprey nest poles. These converted telegraph poles were a big success and by 1989 there were over 60 breeding pairs. The numbers are still increasing.

Above: Ospreys prefer high nesting sites – usually on top of pine trees, but a telegraph pole will do! Left: A female osprey on a man-made nest site. Osprey poles make ideal 'trees' for nesting.

WILDSIDE WATCH

You may not have birds of prey nesting in your back garden but you can help other species.
● Buy or make a nest box. It will attract all sorts of small birds.
● Encourage birds to feed in your back garden. Put out nuts, bread or bird seed in the winter. Keep a record of the species that you see.
● Don't collect birds' eggs.

The deepest lake in the world

LAKE BAIKAL in the Soviet Union is the deepest lake anywhere in the world. Including the layer of silt on the bottom, the actual depth from the surface to the bedrock is 7 km (4.5 miles), seven times as deep as the Grand Canyon. This huge lake, which is bigger than Belgium and 25 million years old, contains an amazing one fifth of the world's fresh water.

Over 1500 types of animal live in and around Lake Baikal. Two thirds of these are found nowhere else on earth. There are seals, birds and fish at the surface while deep in the lake live strange freshwater shrimps and transparent fish. Local people rely on the lake for food and water.

Baikal under threat

THIS HUGE LAKE has its problems. Unlike America's Great Lakes, the Baikal area is still mostly wilderness, but agriculture and industry are putting a stop to that.

When surrounding forests are logged, soil and silt are washed into the lake and its rivers. Timber transported on the lake sometimes sinks. This decays and the bacteria in the wood use up the oxygen in the water. Luckily, felling around the lake has been banned.

But there are still worse problems. There are a hundred factories on the shores of Baikal and the rivers that flow in to it, and you can guess where their waste goes! Millions of tonnes of mercury, zinc and other highly poisonous substances are flushed straight into the water. One particular factory to date has poured 1.5 billion cubic metres of industrial waste into it.

The Green movement is growing in Russia. Their main aim is to save Siberia's unique 'sacred lake' from industrial pollution.

The western coast of Lake Baikal. Parts of the lake have been polluted by chemicals which end up in the fish and lakeside birds.

Lake Michigan
This North American lake (see page 38) is about 300 m (1000 ft) deep. Lake Baikal is more than five times as deep as this, not including the layer of silt on the bottom.

Lake Baikal
Its immense depth means that it holds as much water as all the American Great Lakes put together.

Factories
Paper pulp factories release poisonous chemicals into the lake.

Air pollution
Chemicals released into the air from factories pollute the snow in winter. In spring when the snow melts, high concentrations of chemicals flow into the lake.

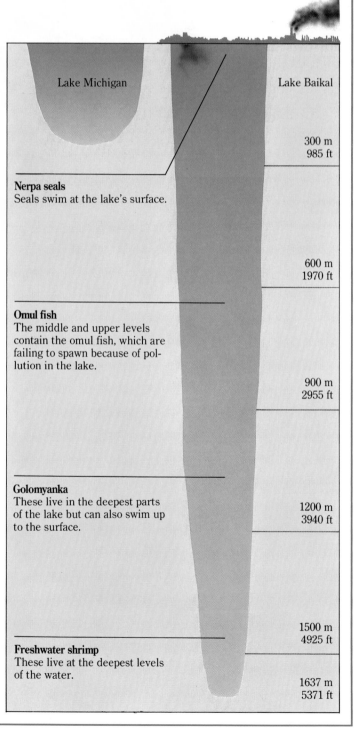

Lake Michigan

Lake Baikal

300 m
985 ft

600 m
1970 ft

900 m
2955 ft

1200 m
3940 ft

1500 m
4925 ft

1637 m
5371 ft

Nerpa seals
Seals swim at the lake's surface.

Omul fish
The middle and upper levels contain the omul fish, which are failing to spawn because of pollution in the lake.

Golomyanka
These live in the deepest parts of the lake but can also swim up to the surface.

Freshwater shrimp
These live at the deepest levels of the water.

Above: A strange transparent fish, the golomyanka, lives in the deepest parts of the lake (see drawing on left), but swims up to the water's surface at night.
Left: Lake Baikal contains 255 types of shrimp. Many live in the deeper parts of the lake (see left). They have enormously long antennae to feel their way around in the black depths.

Freshwater seals

THE NERPA SEAL lives only in the waters of Lake Baikal and is still hunted by local people for fur and meat. There are 70,000 seals on the lake and 5000 are culled each year. This is strictly controlled and hunters are not the main problem.

Thousands of Baikal's seals have died from the same virus that devastated the North Sea's common seals in 1988 and 1989. It may be linked to pollution. The fish eaten by the seals, particularly the omul, bizarre scaleless fish, are contaminated with pollutants from lakeside factories. These poisons build up in the seals and may weaken their resistance to the disease.

Nerpa seals are unique to Lake Baikal. They have been affected by a virus that may be linked to pollution.

WILDSIDE WATCH

You may never have heard of Lake Baikal before but every country has lakes suffering from industrial pollution. You can help put things right.
● If you see pollution from a factory, contact your local conservation organisation. They might be able to campaign to get the pollution controlled.
● Making paper is a highly polluting process. Reduce pollution (and save trees) by using recycled paper.

Rebirth of a lake

THE GREAT LAKES in North America – Lakes Ontario, Erie, Huron, Michigan and Superior – make up the largest body of fresh water on earth. Lake Superior is still a very wild area, home to wildfowl, wolves and moose. Lake Erie in contrast has suffered from pollution, from industry and people.

After years of effort to clean up the heavily polluted lakes, the water is improving. But, there are invisible toxic chemicals which continue to poison the water, affecting the wildlife and the 60 million people who live near these great lakes.

Marine invaders

THEY CAME FROM the sea! They sucked the blood of living fish! They invaded the lakes!

No, not a horror film introduction but a description of sea lampreys. These eel-like marine fish invaded the lakes via the Welland Canal which connects Lake Erie with Lake Ontario and the sea. They spread throughout the lakes, feeding on trout and whitefish, and caused a huge decline in the lakes' native fish which was speeded up by overfishing by the human population. As in all good horror films, the evil lamprey was virtually wiped out by the 1970s. But small numbers are still there, growing faster and larger ...

The sea lamprey attaches itself to fish with its mouth like a mini vampire! The lamprey bores into the fish's flesh with its rough tongue and drinks its blood.

Cleaning up the lakes

IN THE 1960s, Lake Erie was pronounced 'dead'. The lake had become a waste dump for the industries and sewage of Detroit and Cleveland. Sewage and detergents caused a huge algal bloom which used up all the lake's oxygen. Dead fish, dead birds and bacteria were the only 'wildlife' to be seen on some areas of the lake. The lake and its life had been killed, the murder weapon – pollution.

Cleaning up the lakes has become a national issue in Canada and the United States. Sewage plants have been improved, phosphate detergents and household cleaners have been banned in many areas, and many factories have reduced the pollution they cause. Today Lake Erie is much cleaner, so people can once again go fishing and swimming in some parts of the lake.

Lake Erie wasn't the only victim: all five lakes suffered from pollution in varying degrees. They now sparkle again, but they are not totally cured. Toxic chemicals are still a big problem, many of them transported in the air, wind-blown from factories far to the south. Invisible and indestructible, these chemicals gradually build up in the bodies of the fish, the birds and even the people.

Birds of the Great Lakes

CANADA GEESE, great blue herons, crested cormorants, American black ducks and bald eagles; the Great Lakes and their shores are home to thousands of birds.

On Lake Ontario, ducks have been helping the Canadian Wildlife Service find out the levels of pollution. Pekin ducks have been released onto an area of the lake next to a steel plant. The ducks feed on lake plants and plankton. Any pollutants in the water collect in the plankton, and are passed up the food chain to the ducks. Within two months, the ducks were found to contain high levels of lead and chemicals. Now the problem has been proved to exist, pollution from the steel plant should be reduced or even stopped.

America's national bird, the bald eagle, can be seen on the shores of the Great Lakes.

Canada geese can be pests as they sometimes eat farm crops in North America and Europe.

Top: Lake Erie was not the only lake to suffer from pollution. Thousands of fish were killed by pollution in Lake Michigan, shown here. Lakes Erie, Michigan and Ontario have some of America's largest industrial cities on their shores.
Above: This nineteenth-century painting shows Lake Superior, the largest single area of fresh water in the world. It was once the home of Red Indians and even today remains very much a natural wilderness compared with the other Great Lakes.

WILDSIDE
WATCH

There are lakes in cities as well as in the countryside, and they are equally important.
● If you see dead fish or birds in a lake report it to a local conservation organisation or environmental health officer. They may have been killed by pollution.
● Lake Erie shows us how lakes can be brought back from the dead. If a lake near you is polluted campaign to get it cleaned up.
● The lamprey caused havoc in the Great Lakes. Make sure you don't introduce alien animals into a particular habitat by releasing unwanted pets or plants into lakes, rivers or ponds.

Soda lakes and hungry hippos

AFRICA IS A LAND of lakes, from volcanic crater lakes in Tanzania to Kenya's lakes of soda. The lakes are home to many animals. Hippos and crocodiles wallow in the water; lions, gazelle and hyena drop for by drinks; storks and flamingoes paddle in the shallows. Many of the lakes are National Parks or reserves and tourists come from all over the world to see Africa's world-famous birds and mammals.

A high-fibre diet

HIPPOPOTAMUSES play a key role in African lakes and rivers. During the day they wallow in the water and at night they head for the banks to graze, eating up to 40kg (88lb) of grass.

The results of such a high-fibre diet are tonnes of hippo dung! This fertilises the lake with half-digested plant matter. Small animals in the water eat the dung, fish eat the small animals and birds eat the fish. The dung and urine supply nitrogen to the water too, encouraging the growth of algae – more food for the food chain.

The hippos also act as lawnmowers, cropping the grass at the lake edge and making ideal breeding sites for ground-nesting pelicans and spoonbills.

Papyrus
Ancient Egyptians made paper from this plant, the papyrus or giant sedge. It is found in African lakes and swamps and like many other water plants can absorb sewage pollution.

Saddlebill stork
These huge storks wade through the water to disturb small fish with their big feet. They then grab the fish as they swim away.

Small fish
Vast numbers of fish feed on the microscopic animals in the waters of the lake.

Hippo dung
This fertilises the water providing food for small aquatic animals, which are the base of the food chain and are in turn eaten by small fish.

Hippopotamus
The common hippo grows up to 4m (13ft) long and can weigh 4 tonnes! They spend most of their time in the water.

Flamingo service stations

LAKE NATRON, Lake Nakuru and other East African soda lakes (so-called because of the chemicals left behind round the lake when the water evaporates) are home to about five million lesser flamingoes. They breed at Lake Natron, where the weather is hot and the water practically sterile. It is perfect for nesting flamingoes as few predators can survive these conditions.

Flamingoes commute to other lakes to feed on algae and shrimps, which they sieve through their beaks. Lake Nakuru is a popular flamingo service station for over 1.5 million birds. It is a National Park and carefully protected. All the soda lakes need to be protected to maintain these vast numbers of flamingoes.

Five million flamingoes live on Africa's soda lakes. Flamingoes like these at Lake Nakuru in Kenya attract thousands of tourists.

Pelicans
Large numbers of pelicans feed and nest on African lakes. Like the hippos pelicans enrich the water with their droppings.

Small cyprinid fish
One small fish actually feeds on the algae growing on the hippo's skin.

A fishy disaster

INTRODUCING ANIMALS or plants to places where they do not occur naturally can have terrible results. Fish from Lake Victoria in Africa are an important source of food for the local people but as the lakeside population increased many of the native species were overfished. To provide more food Nile perch and freshwater sardines were released into the lake.

Unfortunately the Nile perch is a fierce predator and it began to eat all the other fish. The perch itself proved hard to catch and the local people did not like its taste. Now many of Lake Victoria's fish have disappeared for ever – down the gullet of this freshwater 'Jaws'.

West African fishermen with Lake Victoria's answer to 'Jaws': a huge Nile perch, which is not a natural inhabitant of the lake and munches vast quantities of native fish.

WILDSIDE WATCH

Many of Africa's animals depend on lakes and waterholes for survival, particularly endangered species such as rhinoceros and elephants.
● We all know not to buy ivory, but watch out for less obvious things made from animals: even hippos' teeth can be used to make carved souvenirs and jewellery.
● Find out what birds visit your local lake, river or wetland. Some may spend part of the year in Africa.

Tiger tales

WHAT ON EARTH are forests doing in a book about wetlands? But this is no mistake. In Bangladesh and India, the melting snow from the Himalayas meets the Indian Ocean, forming a vast forested swamp, a halfway house between fresh and salt water. This huge wilderness of mangrove forest, swamp and marsh is the Sunderbans, which means 'beautiful forest'. Mangroves are tropical trees with enormous roots, and this is the biggest mangrove forest in the world.

Strange and dangerous creatures inhabit the mangroves: cobras and crocodiles, deer and river dolphins, turtles and tigers and even the mudskipper, a fish that can walk on land!

The endangered deer

IT'S EASY TO GET international support for schemes to save large popular mammals like tigers and elephants. For smaller animals that people have never heard of, getting support and money for conservation is much more difficult. The brow-antlered deer, or sangai, was once common in India's swamps and wetlands. But, hunted for meat and sport, only one herd now survives. Their final swamp home has been made a National Park, a last refuge for one of the world's rarest deer.

Only one herd of the rare brow-antlered deer remains, although it was once common in India's swamps.

Tiger! Tiger!

IN THE 1970S, the tiger was saved from imminent extinction by 'Operation Tiger', an international campaign by the Worldwide Fund for Nature. Operation Tiger set up reserves to protect this magnificent big cat and hunting tigers for sport and their skins was banned. By 1990 there were an estimated 5000 tigers in Asia.

The Bengal tiger is doing particularly well in the Sunderbans. There are thought to be over 660 tigers there, the largest concentration on earth. They hunt deer, wild pig, fish and even crabs, and are strong swimmers. Operation Tiger has worked but the local people are paying the price. In 1981, 50 people were eaten in the Indian Sunderbans alone.

A novel way to stop tigers lunching on people has been devised in the Sunderbans tiger reserve. The park rangers and fishermen wear human masks on the back of their heads. This baffles the tigers as they always attack from behind. Human dummies are also placed in the park. When a tiger attacks a dummy, it receives a 300 volt electric shock, enough to put it off a human diet for life. These simple solutions have cut the number of deaths by about half.

Above right: Tigers are good swimmers. In the Sunderbans they hunt swamp deer, pigs, fish and crabs and by the look of this one even the occasional cameraman!
Right: Tigers nearly always attack from behind. These fishermen in the Sunderbans are not taking any chances – their garish masks will, they hope, prevent them from becoming a tiger snack!

Underwater sheepdogs

THE SUNDERBANS is vital for the local people as well as wildlife. Mangroves provide firewood and spawning grounds for fish, an important part of the local diet.

The local fishermen have a strange method of fishing, using trained otters rather as farmers use sheepdogs. The otters are kept on leads attached to the boat. When the men spot a shoal of fish the otters are released. These expert underwater swimmers then herd the shoal towards the fishermen's nets, like sheep to a pen. The fisherman pulls in his full nets and the otters are rewarded with a fish supper.

A Sunderbans fisherman with his specially trained fishing otters.

WILDSIDE WATCH

Countries like India and Bangladesh may seem far away but we should still help them protect their environment.
● Join organisations battling to help wildlife in other countries.
● In some countries you can still buy skins and souvenirs made from endangered animals. Would you be tempted?
● Other big cats such as Asiatic cheetahs, snow leopards and the Asiatic lion are threatened. Why not do a school project on endangered cats?

Down in the swamps

THE DIFFERENCE BETWEEN a marsh and a swamp
is that marshes are wet grasslands, but swamps,
like America's famous Atchafalaya swamp in
Louisiana, are waterlogged forests packed with
cypress and tupelo trees – perfect habitat for
crocodiles and alligators. There are 22 types
of alligator and crocodile ranging from the 7 m
(23 ft) salt water crocodile to the 1.45 m (4 ft
10 in) dwarf caiman.

'Gators and crocs are under attack as swamps
all over the world are vanishing. At least three
species are faced with extinction from poaching.
The American alligator however, is doing well –
it's even invading swimming pools in Florida!

Alligator alert!

THE AMERICAN ALLIGATOR is back with a vengeance. These
3 m (10 ft) long reptiles live in the southern United States.
There are thought to be over a million in Florida alone! In
fact, local people regard them as a nuisance. There are
'gators in backyards, 'gators on golfcourses, 'gators are
even ending up in people's swimming pools. So what do you
do if you find yourself doing backstroke with an alligator?
Call in the official alligator nuisance patrol to remove it!

American alligator numbers in Florida are stable but despite
their success they are still vulnerable, not from the effects of
hunting, but from houses and people invading their territory.

Right: An alligator basks in an American swamp.

Reptiles at risk

THE CHINESE ALLIGATOR is not the only
reptile in danger. Almost all of the 22
species of crocodile and alligator are
threatened by poaching, disturbance
or destruction of their river homes.
The false gavial, black caiman and
estuarine or salt-water crocodile are
all endangered. The broad-nosed
caiman, Philippines crocodile and the
Siamese crocodile are facing extinction. Unless drastic action is taken to
set up protected areas, stop hunting,
or breed these large reptiles in captivity many species could disappear by
the year 2000.

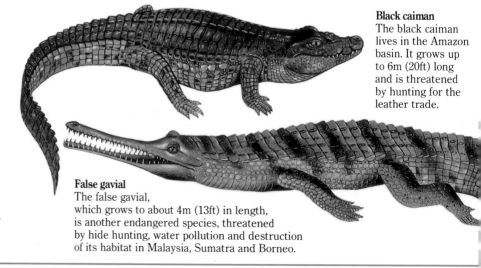

Black caiman
The black caiman
lives in the Amazon
basin. It grows up
to 6m (20ft) long
and is threatened
by hunting for the
leather trade.

False gavial
The false gavial,
which grows to about 4m (13ft) in length,
is another endangered species, threatened
by hide hunting, water pollution and destruction
of its habitat in Malaysia, Sumatra and Borneo.

The alligator café

ALLIGATORS play a very important role in rivers and swamps. They dig holes in the banks of ponds, streams or under the roots of a tree. These holes fill with water and act as 'cafeterias' providing food and drink for other wildlife as well as alligators. During the dry season mammals, birds, and insects quench their thirst at these 'gator-made water-holes. Without the alligators many animals would die from lack of water.

Plants and insects move into the pools, providing food for fish, birds and lizards. Alligators and birds eat the fish. If the alligators disappear the whole swamp is affected.

An alligator food chain

1 Alligators dig their very own 'gator holes to live in.

2 These holes are an ideal home for other water creatures – insects and fish.

3 The insects provide food for the fish and the fish in turn are eaten by the alligators.

Breeding reptiles in captivity

THE CHINESE ALLIGATOR is the only alligator found outside America. Unlike its American relative it is critically endangered in the wild. To try to protect the species from extinction New York's Bronx Zoo has been breeding these alligators in captivity. The scheme has been so successful that in 1989 there were 88 Chinese alligators in the United States.

Captive breeding stops animals from disappearing entirely, but it is no replacement for conserving animals in the wild. Relatives of the Chinese alligator have been on earth for almost 200 million years. If undisturbed areas of its natural habitat are not protected from farming and pollution it will only exist as a zoo curiosity.

A rare Chinese alligator hatches in New York's Bronx Zoo, where a captive-breeding scheme is in operation to increase the numbers in the species.

WILDSIDE WATCH

So reptiles aren't cute and cuddly but they are still amazing animals that need your help!
● Discover more about the less appealing animals that are threatened.
● Find out the difference between alligators and crocodiles.
● See if you can find reptile skins for sale in local stores, as handbags, shoes and souvenirs.
● Don't be tempted to buy a crocodile or alligator as a pet. They need expert care and attention.

Estuarine crocodile
This grows up to 9m (30ft) long, making it the largest reptile on earth. Its habitat in Australia and South-east Asia is being reduced and it is also hunted for its skin.

The changing Everglades

EVERYONE HAS HEARD of the Everglades, a vast area of cypress swamp, mangrove and marsh at the southern tip of Florida. This famous wetland is a haven for some amazing wildlife.

Three hundred types of bird, 25 mammals and 60 types of reptile can be found in the Everglades. Manatees, Florida panthers, bald eagles and American crocodiles are just some of Florida's endangered animals. They have all found refuge in the Everglades National Park.

The swamps were once an untamed wilderness, but not any more. Everyone wants to holiday in or retire to America's 'Sunshine State' and that means the Everglades are threatened on all sides from agriculture, drainage schemes, buildings and people.

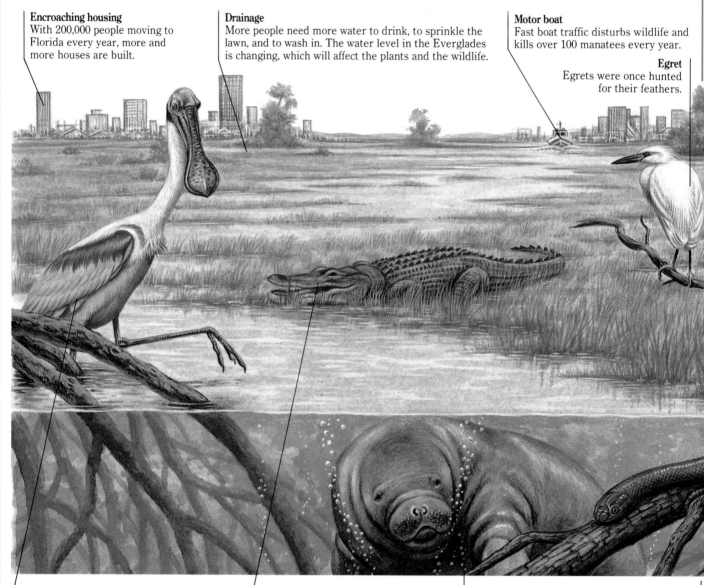

Encroaching housing
With 200,000 people moving to Florida every year, more and more houses are built.

Drainage
More people need more water to drink, to sprinkle the lawn, and to wash in. The water level in the Everglades is changing, which will affect the plants and the wildlife.

Motor boat
Fast boat traffic disturbs wildlife and kills over 100 manatees every year.

Egret
Egrets were once hunted for their feathers.

Spoonbill
The roseate spoonbill lives in coastal lagoons of the southern United States. Its bill, like a long wide spatula, is just right for sweeping up small fish, frogs and aquatic insects from the water.

American crocodile
Unlike the alligator, the American crocodile is only found in very small numbers in Florida. It is still endangered but not declining in numbers.

Manatee
The manatee is an endangered species. They grow up to 1600kg (3500lb) and eat about 50kg (110lb) of water plants a day. There is now a manatee sanctuary on Crystal river where diving and boats are banned.

Florida snail kite
This bird of prey is only found in Florida. It feeds solely on a small water snail. As the water levels change the snails disappear, and so do the kites.

Birds of a feather

IN THE MID-NINETEENTH century, an amazing 2.5 million birds could be found in the Everglades. But that soon changed: in the 1880s, every fashionable woman had to have a feathered hat. The hunters moved in to the Everglades and shot thousands of blue herons, snowy egrets and ibis to supply feathers for the hat trade. Fortunately, plume hunting was eventually banned, but not before half the Everglades birds had been wiped out for the sake of fashion.

The numbers of birds began to build up again but this increase was short-lived. The twentieth century brought its own set of problems. Just when they thought it was safe to go back into the Everglades, the birds were threatened again, this time by the destruction of their nesting and feeding areas and changes in water levels. The numbers of wading birds in the Everglades has dropped by an incredible 95 per cent in the last 125 years.

This little blue heron would once have decorated a fashionable Victorian hat.

Going, going, gone

THE FLORIDA PANTHER, found only in the Southern United States, is in big trouble. The current wild population is thought to be only 30 to 50. Within the National Park there are no male panthers and the females have suffered from mercury poisoning – from an unknown source. Panthers need large territories to hunt and although the park is big, it may not be big enough to save the species. There are plans to breed panthers in captivity and release them into the Everglades. This may be the only way to stop this rare big cat from extinction.

The endangered Florida panther. Only 30 to 50 remain in the wild, mostly within the Everglades National Park.

Indigo snakes
These 2m (6ft 6in) long snakes were once common. They have vanished from many areas because of destruction of their habitat for housing and development.

WILDSIDE WATCH

The Everglades are not the only wetlands under threat from drainage and disturbance. You don't have to be a politician or professional conservationist to help the world's wetlands.
● **We all like to spend days out or holidays near water. If you go walking, boating, swimming or windsurfing, try not to disturb the wildlife.**
● **Be careful not to leave litter in or near water. Dispose of it properly.**

Riches of nature or riches for man?

The Pantanal in Brazil is a vast wetland – three times the size of Belgium and home to crocodiles, otters, capybara and thousands of birds.

THE PANTANAL IN BRAZIL is the largest wetland in the world. Jaguar, capybara, crocodiles and at least 650 types of bird live in an area of swamp and flood plain three times the size of Belgium. It is home to many endangered animals such as the maned wolf, giant otter and the giant anteater.

For the local people, the Pantanal provides fish and farm land; it hides deposits of gold; and for many it's a place to hunt for rare and valuable animals.

All over the world, the great wetlands like the Pantanal and Kakadu in Australia are suffering from uranium and gold fever. These huge wetlands hide valuable minerals and mining them brings people, roads, pollution and conflict. But that is not all: there are problems with tourism, hunting, and overfishing as well.

The skin trade

THERE ARE 50 different species of reptile in the Pantanal. The largest and most spectacular is the caiman crocodile. This crocodile has a problem – its skin. One million crocs are killed each year to make handbags and shoes. They have little chance to survive against the poachers, who use speed boats, automatic weapons, and even small aeroplanes.

It is not just the crocodiles that are under fire. In 1985, a shipment of poached skins was confiscated at Brazil's major airport. It contained 70,000 jaguar, snake and caiman skins, bound for the European fashion houses.

Some of the Pantanal's other creatures do escape with their lives, but not their freedom. Hyacinth macaws, large beautiful parrots, are smuggled out of the Pantanal, to sell as pets. In European pet shops, a pair will sell for at least £7000, and now only 3000 remain in the wild.

Above: Crocodiles and alligators can end up as tasteless tourist souvenirs.
Right: A broad-nosed caiman 'smiles' at the camera. It may not be smiling long. In Brazil, one million of its relatives have finished up as handbags and shoes.

Gold mining and pollution

AT THE EDGE OF the Pantanal, gold fever has made some people rich – and left the Pantanal polluted.

Tonnes of silt suffocate the rivers as they are dredged for gold. The gold miners also use poisonous mercury to separate the gold from the soil. And guess where the mercury ends up? In the rivers flowing into the Pantanal, poisoning the fish and entering the wetland food chain. Two rivers are now completely devoid of life because of mercury pollution.

Despite the problems from mining and poaching, conservationists are hoping to save the Pantanal from further destruction.

Gold fever! The mining of gold pollutes wetlands like the Pantanal, particularly where poisonous mercury is used to separate out the gold.

An Australian wetland

KAKADU IS AUSTRALIA'S most famous national park. Flood plains, rivers, creeks and billabongs spread over an area the size of Wales. Kakadu is a World Heritage Site which means that it is internationally recognised as being a 'wonder of the world' like the Grand Canyon and the Pyramids. It has some strange inhabitants. Frill-necked lizards, black wallabies and spiny anteaters live here, with rare hooded parrots and a new species of marsupial mouse discovered in 1989.

But, like the Pantanal, Kakadu's rare and new species are at war with miners. Areas of the park are scarred with mines, where uranium is mined for the nuclear industry.

The Ranger uranium mine on the edge of Kakadu National Park in Australia's Northern Territory, where parts of the wetland have been destroyed.

WILDSIDE WATCH

There are weird and wonderful wetlands all over the world. The animals that live there need all the help they can get.

● Support organisations fighting to protect wetlands. The World Wide Fund for Nature and the International Union for the Conservation of Nature are hard at work.
● Help stop trade in animal skins and souvenirs by not buying them! Photographs are a much nicer souvenir of a visit.
● Having a pet at home is great but exotic pets, such as parrots or lizards, may have been taken from the wild. Only buy from a reputable source and check it isn't imported.

Wild horses,

ALL WETLANDS need protecting. Man obviously plays a big part in this but animals can be conservationists too. Large grazing animals such as cattle, sheep and horses can create areas which make a suitable habitat for other wildlife. In Scotland, for example, pintail ducks like to nest in fields where cattle have grazed; in Sweden, conservationists are using ponies and rabbits to create an ideal home for large blue butterflies. In France, the herds of wild horses are conserving Europe's most famous marsh – the Camargue.

Conserving the marsh

THE CAMARGUE is a huge reserve of marsh and lagoons in the delta of the great river Rhone in southern France. It is one of the largest wetlands in Europe. Its wild white horses, black bulls and water birds, and especially its colony of flamingoes, are world famous. Thousands of tourists visit the area every year, attracted by the abundance of wildlife.

Large herbivores can cause a great deal of damage to wetlands by eating and trampling on delicate plants and driving out wildlife. But in the Camargue the horses are 'marsh conservationists'. Parts of this unique area have been created and are maintained by these four-legged lawn-mowers. If they were removed, the reserve would be taken over by scrub and trees. So how do they do this?

In the parts of the reserve where these big vegetarians are absent reedbeds grow. Bearded tits, bitterns, and marsh harriers live in these areas. But where horses graze, the reeds are gradually replaced by shorter rushes and underwater plants. This makes open areas of marsh and water, ideal for ducks, waders and flamingoes.

wild places

The threats

THE CAMARGUE is protected as a national park. It is carefully looked after and prized both locally and internationally.

On the edges of the Camargue however it can be a different story. The flamingoes have to share their space with heavy industry; illegal hunting still goes on and pollution enters the water from industry further up on the river Rhone. The crowds of tourists may be affecting areas of the park too – sometimes the wild horses are chased across the marshes and frightened so that visitors can get the perfect 'galloping' photo!

Above: Flamingoes feed in the shadow of a factory on the edge of the Camargue.
Far left: The wild white horses are perhaps the Camargue's most famous inhabitants. They are particularly important in maintaining the ecological balance of the marsh.
Left: A scientist marks a grey heron chick in the Camargue. Marking and ringing is rather like giving a bird an identity bracelet. If the bird is recaptured or found dead the mark or ring will enable scientists to find out where it comes from.

WILDSIDE WATCH

Even small areas of wetland are important for birds and insects, especially if there is a marsh in the middle of a big city.
● If there is a marsh near you find out what lives there.
● Set up or join a group to look after a local marsh or wetland. It's not as difficult as it may seem and you may even get rare species like great crested newts breeding there.

Draining the marshes

IMAGINE FLYING thousands of kilometres on holiday, only to find that when you arrive, your destination has disappeared. That's what happens to thousands of migrating birds; they fly to their winter wetlands to find it has all gone down the drain. The marshland homes of otters, reptiles and insects as well as birds are dwindling every year and the cause is drainage.

Marshes are drained to prevent flooding and to provide farmland. But removing the water means that the animals and plants of the wetlands have to move out. Swallowtail butterflies, bitterns and the rare whooping crane have all suffered, victims of the retreating marshland.

Drainage ditches
Marshes are drained either to provide dry land for pasture or crops, or to supply water for farmland.

Housing
As the human population expands, more and more houses encroach on to the marsh.

Bearded tit

Butterflies at risk

BUTTERFLIES are at risk. The beautiful swallowtail butterflies are particularly vulnerable. In Asia, the swallowtails' problem is that they are too beautiful. Huge numbers of these butterfly beauty queens are collected and shipped out, alive to zoos and other collections, or dead to make souvenirs. In Taiwan, 500 million butterflies a year are transformed into bookmarks, tablemats and coasters.

In England, the problem is drainage. The swallowtail is found throughout Europe, but in England it lives only in the Norfolk Broads. It is England's biggest and rarest butterfly. The swallowtail is extremely fussy. It will only lay its eggs on milk parsley, a plant which grows in fens and marshes. When marshes are drained the milk parsley dies out. The swallowtails have nowhere to lay their eggs, the caterpillars have nowhere to feed, so the butterflies die out.

If marshes continue to disappear other butterflies like the rare European marsh fritillary may end up vanishing too.

Black sedge | Bittern | Milk parsley

Reed-beds
Reed-beds are the nesting sites for many birds such as bitterns and bearded tits.

The life cycle of the swallowtail butterfly
1 Butterfly laying eggs
In early summer the swallowtail butterfly lays its eggs on milk parsley.

2 Caterpillar
Caterpillars hatch after a week and feed on the parsley.

Dragonfly

Marshes are home to many insect species, such as dragonflies. Drainage destroys their breeding sites, a serious problem if the insects are rare.

Bulrush

The booming bittern

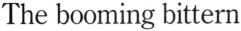

THE BITTERN is a shy member of the heron family. There are 16 different species in the world ranging from the American bittern to the black bittern from China.

In Britain, the bittern was once a common sight. But the drainage of marshes and fens has resulted in the loss of reedbeds, the bitterns' favourite nesting sites. With the added problems of water pollution and disturbance from boats, the secretive bitterns are disappearing. But their reedbed refuges are now nature reserves, hopeful news for the 20–25 pairs that by 1990 were still there.

The bittern is perfectly camouflaged in its reed-bed nest.

Whooping it up!

CONSERVATION STORIES aren't all full of doom and gloom. One of the world's rarest birds, the whooping crane, has been brought back from the brink of extinction. Fifty years ago, there were only 16 of these birds left. They had almost disappeared because their natural home had been drained, ploughed up, and invaded by people.

One group of wild whooping cranes remains and they are now heavily protected. Their nesting site in Canada is a national park, and their winter feeding ground in Texas is a wildlife refuge. Due to careful protection the population in 1990 was 136, and increasing every year. A good reason for the cranes to whoop it up!

Whooping cranes at their winter holiday location in Aransas National Wildlife Refuge in Texas.

3 Pupa

After a month of solid eating the caterpillars turn into pupae.

4 Adult butterfly

Within three weeks the adults emerge. Some live until the end of the summer, some hibernate and emerge the following spring.

WILDSIDE WATCH

All sorts of butterflies are at risk. You can help protect them.
● Attract butterflies to your garden by planting buddleia, iceplant, or honeysuckle.
● Local conservation groups are always interested in information on what butterflies are around. Choose an area (a garden, field, or park) and record what butterflies are there.
● Souvenirs made from butterflies may look very pretty, but thousands of butterflies are caught and killed to make them. Check where the butterflies came from if you are tempted.
● Whooping cranes are evidence that conservation does work! If you are interested in saving birds you could join an organisation (see page 63).

Plants, peat and plovers

BOGS - ON THE SURFACE these weird wetlands look really boring. They're soggy, flat and empty. Or are they . . . ? Peat bogs (or mires) found all over the world are home to some unique and endangered wildlife. Carnivorous plants eat insects in American bogs; orang-utans hang out in the huge peat swamp forests of Indonesia; and the rare Greenland white-fronted geese visit the bogs of Ireland. Bogs abound in Canada, Trinidad, the USSR, and most of Europe, particularly Finland. Don't be fooled by appearances, bogs are amazing places, but they are in danger in every country. They are dug up or drained to provide farmland, fuel, wood and fertiliser for your garden.

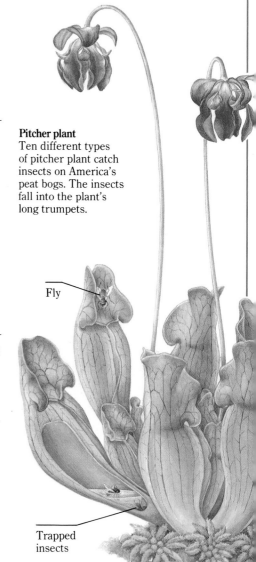

Pitcher plant
Ten different types of pitcher plant catch insects on America's peat bogs. The insects fall into the plant's long trumpets.

Fly

Trapped insects

Down in the bogs

SO WHY ARE peat bogs so interesting? Firstly, they are packed with some pretty unusual plants. The main plant on a peat bog is sphagnum moss. It acts like a huge bath sponge soaking up litres of water so effectively that Red Indians used dried sphagnum moss as babies' nappies.

Other bog plants feast on animals. Pitcher plants in America entice flies with a wonderful smell. The fly slips down into the plant's bell and is trapped and digested. Yum! Other hungry plants include giant sundews which catch their prey using plant 'superglue'. But not all bog plants bite: many rare orchids can be found growing on peatland too.

Waterlogged bogs are ideal places for aquatic insects and biting flies, not man's best friends but perfect food for birds and frogs. Other insects include giant hawk moths and dragonflies.

Larger bog-loving animals include deer, hares, lemmings and voles. But bogs are really for the birds. The peatland provides nest sites, a place for a winter holiday, or somewhere to hunt for lunch for many different birds. Geese, divers, plovers, short-eared owls, merlins, and even golden eagles will hunt the boglands.

For peat's sake!

WHEN YOU BITE into a home-grown vegetable or your mum and dad buy a sack of peat from a garden centre, you may be helping to destroy a peat bog. In Britain, peatlands have been dug up to supply bags of peat for millions of back gardens.

Britain has lost 96 per cent of its peat bogs in the last 150 years. Scotland's bogs are disappearing under fir tree plantations and in Canada and the USSR peat is dug up for fuel.

But the destruction of bogs doesn't just affect the wildlife. Peat stores tonnes of carbon dioxide. When the bog is dug up, this is released and adds to the greenhouse effect.

The destruction of a bog. This bulldozer is destroying a peat bog in Wales.

The culprit! Many peat bogs end up in our back gardens.

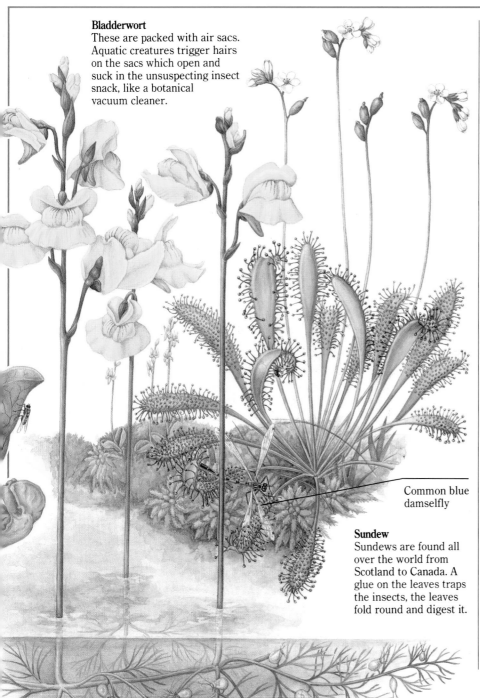

Bladderwort
These are packed with air sacs. Aquatic creatures trigger hairs on the sacs which open and suck in the unsuspecting insect snack, like a botanical vacuum cleaner.

Common blue damselfly

Sundew
Sundews are found all over the world from Scotland to Canada. A glue on the leaves traps the insects, the leaves fold round and digest it.

Trapped aquatic insect

Birds beware!

PEAT BOGS ARE perfect nesting sites for birds. Scotland's 'Flow country', a huge area of undisturbed bog, is Britain's most important area for breeding moorland birds. The beautiful red-throated diver (or loon) which is found in North America and Europe nests on small lochs in the Flows together with golden plovers, Arctic skuas, and short-eared owls.

Large areas have been ploughed up and planted with fir trees, destroying the birds' nesting sites. Luckily conservationists have stopped further damage. So bogs do have friends!

Curlews, plovers and divers nest on peat bogs. If the bogs are destroyed they have nowhere to nest.

A red-throated diver testing the water in Scotland's Flow country.

WILDSIDE WATCH

You may never visit a peat bog, but the animals and plants there need your help.
● If you or your family are keen gardeners find out what companies are destroying peat bogs and don't buy their products.
● Try to get gardening relatives to buy an alternative to peat. There are plenty made from recycled waste and vegetables!
● Why not buy a carnivorous plant? They are excellent at fly catching, and much better for the environment than chemical fly sprays.

Man-made wetlands

WITH THE NUMBER of natural wetlands decreasing every year, man-made wetlands are a welcome refuge for wildlife. Some birds will make their home wherever there is water so canals, reservoirs, even sewage treatment plants can be excellent places to go wildlife watching.

These man-made wetlands are not always created intentionally. In America and Europe gravel pits often fill with water to form networks of lakes perfect for recreation and wildlife. Some species, like the great crested grebe, have even been saved from extinction by these accidental wetlands.

Unexpected wetlands

DIGGING GRAVEL for concrete is one of the few industries that leaves behind something beneficial to wildlife.

In the United States a billion tonnes of gravel are used every year. If conservationists step in, the pits can be made into excellent nature reserves. In Crookston, Minnesota, a gravel pit nature reserve is home to spotted sandpipers, eastern kingbirds, wood duck and over 35 other types of bird. There are deer, raccoons, muskrats, skunks, woodchucks and even moose.

In Britain, great crested grebes were saved from extinction by gravel pits. A hundred years ago the birds were almost wiped out, their feathers used for hats and fans, but once hunting was banned the pits provided undisturbed areas where they could breed in peace and they are now a common species. Sixty per cent of the grebe population live on flooded gravel pits, together with dragonflies, reed warblers and plovers.

Above right: Eastern kingbirds are common visitors to American gravel pit nature areas.
Right: Like the Everglades' birds in Florida, the great crested grebe was almost wiped out in Britain by the Victorian hat trade. They are now common, nesting on reservoirs and gravel pits.

Wildfowl waterholes

RESERVOIRS and sewage works are ideal refuges for waterfowl. If reservoirs are rich in plants and food huge numbers of ducks such as mallard, goldeneye, and shoveller move in. Smew (a type of duck) fly thousands of kilometres from Scandinavia and Russia to join other migratory birds spending the winter season on London's reservoirs.

Sewage treatment plants may sound unappealing but they are ideal for birds too. Worms and other tasty morsels can be found in the sewage-enriched mud, and dunlin, ringed plover, redshank and snipe are all regular visitors to the sewage snack bars.

Shoveler and pintail duck congregate to feed on an inner city reservoir.

Canals for wildlife

UP TO 500 types of insect, 15 types of fish, 130 birds, 30 butterflies, 15 dragon and damsel flies and 100 water plants can be found on Northern European canals. Not a bad record!

Canals are also habitat for people; we use them for fishing, boating, and water sports. The Basingstoke canal in Hampshire, England has been cleared and restored by local enthusiasts, but one section of the canal remains closed: a tunnel that houses roosting long-eared, Daubenton's, whiskered and natterer's bats. Many canal users would like to see the tunnel open to boats, but conservationists fear this would disturb the bats. A balanced use of the canal will ensure that bats, other wildlife and people can exist side by side.

Left: The controversial tunnel on the Basingstoke Canal, where six species of bats live.
Below: A long-eared bat tucks into its supper – a moth. There are 951 species of bat in the world and many of them roost in man-made 'caves' such as tunnels, houses or churches.

WILDSIDE **WATCH**

Derelict wastelands can sometimes be made into nature reserves.
● If there are any near you, contact a local conservation group.
● See how many birds live on a local reservoir or other man-made wetland. Keep a record.
● If you are keen on getting your feet wet, join a local organisation clearing up derelict canals – your library should have information.

Your own water reserve

VILLAGE, farm or garden ponds are all small wetlands, perfect refuges for wildlife. American ponds are home to bullfrogs that can jump nine times their own length, giant salamanders, terrapins and muskrats. In European ponds, pond skaters speed skate on the water surface, diving spiders use bubbles of air like scuba apparatus and dragonfly larvae resemble mysterious aliens from a science fiction movie.

But ponds have problems too. They are disappearing at an alarming rate. They are neglected, drained, used as dumps and polluted.

Damsels and dragons in distress

DRAGONFLIES and damselflies are the aerial acrobats of wetlands. These insects are nature's pollution monitors, as they live only near unpolluted and healthy ponds. Pollution stops the eggs from hatching and reduces the oxygen in the water, killing the larvae.

If a pond is drained, the dragonflies have nowhere to feed or breed. Garden ponds are becoming more and more important as refuges for homeless dragonflies.

The life cycle of a dragonfly
1 Dragonflies scatter their eggs over the water surface. Some even lay their eggs inside water plants.
2 The larvae or nymphs hatch and spend between one and five years under water. They are fierce hunters, feeding on other animals such as worms.
3 When the nymph is ready to change into an adult it climbs up a plant stem, the skin splits and the adult emerges.

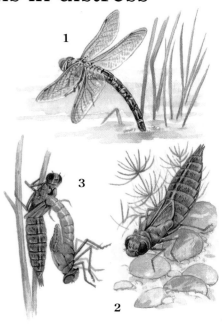

Yellow iris | Dragonfly

White water lily
These beautiful lilies are very sensitive to pollution. They cannot grow on polluted water.

Pond skaters
These common insects are fierce carnivores. They speed skate across the pond surface catching other insects.

Canadian pond weed
This weed is commonly sold in pet shops to decorate aquariums. It is not native to Europe but is now spreading through ponds and rivers.

Mayfly larva
Mayfly, like dragonflies, lay their eggs in water. The larvae develop under water and then climb up a plant stem. The larval skin splits and the flying adult emerges. Many mayfly adults live for only one day – long enough to mate and lay eggs.

Make your own pond

DIG A HOLE in a suitable site in your garden, making sure that the sides are sloped. Place a pond liner in the hole. These can be bought from gardening shops.

Fill the pond with water and cover the edges of the liner with turf or stones. Leave the water for two days to allow the chemicals in the tap water to evaporate.

Stock the pond with water plants such as water milfoil and pondweeds. In the shallow area around the edges, plant reeds, iris and water mint in soil-filled hessian bags. All sorts of insects and birds will visit your new wetland.

Stocking your new pond with water plants such as iris will ensure that it looks pretty and will attract insects.

Damselfly
Damselflies are smaller and much more delicate than dragonflies and they hold their wings along their body when they rest.

Tadpoles
Frog and toad spawn and tadpoles are common in ponds. If you collect tadpoles always put the young frogs and toads back in the pond.

Toad spawn
Toad spawn and frog spawn look very different. Frog spawn is found in a huge mass whereas toad spawn is laid in long ribbons with two parallel layers of eggs.

Newts that stop bulldozers!

IT'S UNLIKELY that you will find a great crested newt in a home-made pond. Once common throughout western Europe, they are now an endangered species. Although common newts, palmate newts and salamanders do well in garden ponds, great crested newts prefer old deep ponds.

But these newts have hidden powers! They can stop bulldozers. In some areas they are so heavily protected, that if they are found on land that is about to be developed, building cannot go ahead. In Cambridgeshire, England, builders even had to construct a tunnel so that these rare newts could reach their traditional breeding pond.

The great crested newt suffered from the loss of ponds. It is still rare in northern Europe.

Water reptiles

TERRAPINS AND SNAKES are common in ponds. One of the largest freshwater terrapins is the alligator snapping turtle. It feeds on fish in ponds from Canada to South America and grows to an amazing 100 kg (220 lb)!

Snakes can also be semi-aquatic, swimming and living in ponds to feed on fish, tadpoles and newts. The European grass snake can be found in undisturbed ponds. Its American cousins spend more time in the water and are known as water snakes.

Paddlers beware: the snapper turtle will snap at most moving objects including an unsuspecting toe!

WILDSIDE WATCH

Ponds need care and attention to keep them healthy.
● **Organise a team of friends to look after a local pond, or join an existing pond-conservation group.**
● **No ponds in your area? Why not make your own?**
● **Persuade your family not to use chemical fertilisers and pesticides. Aphids and slugs provide food for birds, toads and ladybirds. If you do need to use chemicals, make sure they are environmentally 'safe'.**

Wetlands not wastelands

ALL OVER THE WORLD people are battling to save the world's lakes, rivers and wetlands. From Austria to Zimbabwe conservationists and governments are starting to protect these globally important sites and their wildlife.

Some sites have been earmarked for special attention by wildlife organisations. These sites contain some very rare species. The Coto Donana reserve in Spain for example, is one of Europe's great wildlife reserves. Some of Europe's most impressive animals live there, including the endangered Spanish lynx and the imperial eagle, but neighbouring tourist resorts and farms are using up the water the wildlife rely on.

There are hundreds of wetlands of international importance such as the Camargue in France, the Pantanal in Brazil, and the Sunderbans in Bangladesh and India. Some are national parks, reserves or wildlife sanctuaries, most are threatened in some way by people. The future of some of the world's rare animals is dependent on the future of wetlands.

LOCATION
Kafue flats, Zambia, Africa
THREATENED SPECIES
Lechwe (a type of antelope)
TOTAL POPULATION
50,000
THREATS
Hunting, the construction of hydro-electric dams

The Kafue flats in Zambia are a vast area of river, swamp and floodplain. Lechwe (pronounced letch-vee) are antelope that are always found near water. They are excellent swimmers. The largest remaining group of these antelope on the Kafue flats are threatened by poaching and two enormous hydro-electric dams on the river, which have interfered with the water levels. There is now a project under way to protect the lechwe.

LOCATION
Coto Donana National Park,
Spain
THREATENED SPECIES
Spanish lynx
TOTAL POPULATION
1000 to 1500
THREATS
Poaching, pesticide pollution,
drainage

Coto Donana is one of the most
valuable wetland sanctuaries
for wildlife in western Europe.
The park consists of marshes,
lagoons, streams and coastal
wetlands. The endangered
Spanish lynx once occurred
throughout Spain, but now only
about 1500 remain, mainly in
the Coto Donana, with a few
scattered in the snowy
mountains of northern Spain.

LOCATION
Florida, particularly the
Everglades National Park
THREATENED SPECIES
Florida snail kite
TOTAL POPULATION
Between 250 and 650 in
Florida
THREATS
Changing water levels reducing
food supplies

The snail kite is a tropical bird
found in the United States, only
in Florida. It feeds entirely on
one other animal, the apple
snail. If water levels change,
the apple snails become scarce
and the kites starve. In years of
drought when more water than
usual is extracted from the
Everglades, numbers can drop
as low as 250.

LOCATION
Sumatran swamp forest
THREATENED SPECIES
White-winged wood duck
TOTAL POPULATION
Estimated at 200
THREATS
Forest destruction

The white-winged wood duck is
one of the most endangered
wildfowl in the world. It lives
on slow-moving rainforest
streams and pools in Asia. It
nests in tree holes close to
swampy ground and is
threatened by swamp forest
destruction.

WILDSIDE
WATCH

Global conservation of
wetlands is a big issue.
You can help in your own
local area but you can
support international
action too.
● Find out what other animals are endangered due
to threats to wetlands.
● Find out if there are any
globally important wetland
areas in your country.
Some internationally
important wetland areas
are known as Ramsar
sites – there are 450 in the
world.
● The World Wide Fund
for Nature runs many
projects to save threat-
ened wetland wildlife.
Wildlife organisations
need your support.

Save the wetlands!

LAKES, RIVERS AND WETLANDS are under threat, but help is at hand, from you!

All over the world young people are helping to protect these places and their wildlife. Children are leading the way, saving endangered animals, stopping pollution and creating homes for frogs and toads. At Mount Bethel School in Georgia, United States, the pupils have made the yard into a perfect wildlife habitat: they have dug a huge pond, planted trees, and made a home for king snakes, butterflies and frogs. All over Europe, North America and Australia children are making their very own refuges for wildlife in their back gardens or at school.

Marshes are being saved too! At Nutfield marsh, in Surrey, England, local volunteers have transformed an overgrown marsh into a haven for wildlife, where even the endangered great crested newt breeds. In Germany, groups of young people are clearing up rivers, turning them into areas pleasant to visit and safe for local wildlife. In Australia, children (and adults) have even stopped huge dams being built!

There are millions of young people doing their bit for the environment. This book will have shown you just how remarkable the wildlife of the world's rivers, lakes and wetlands can be, and how vital it is to save these areas. Protecting these habitats for the future is up to you.

Above right: The school yard at Mount Bethel School, Georgia, in the United States. The children have made a perfect habitat for wetland wildlife.
Below: Rafts are filled with plants to encourage birds to nest on urban lakes or reservoirs.

These children are learning about conserving pond life with the naturalist David Bellamy in the Surrey Wildlife Trust nature reserve at Nower Wood.

Children clear dead plants from a city wetland. Conservation activities of this sort are being carried out by young people all over the world.

Useful addresses

There are many organisations you can join or contact. It's a good idea to send a stamped, self-addressed envelope when you ask for information.

Carnivorous Plant Society
Mr & Mrs D. Watts
174 Baldwins Lane
Croxley Green
Herts WD3 3LQ
Provides advice on how to grow insect-eating plants.

Council for the Protection of Rural England (CPRE)
Warwick House
25 Buckingham Palace Road
London SW1W 0PP
Campaigns to protect the countryside against development.

Fauna and Flora Preservation Society (FFPS)
79–83 North Street
Brighton
Sussex BN1 1ZA
Campaigns to protect areas with wild plants and flowers.

Friends of the Earth
26–28 Underwood Street
London N1 7JQ
Campaigns to protect the environment.

Greenpeace
30–31 Islington Green
London N1 8XE
Campaigns to protect the world's seas and the creatures in them.

Nature Conservancy Council
Northminster House
Peterborough
Cambs PE1 1UA
Campaigns to protect Britain's countryside and wildlife.

WATCH Clubs
c/o Royal Society for Nature Conservation (RSNC)
The Green
Witham Park
Waterside South
Lincoln LN5 7JR
Young people's conservation group that campaigns to protect the countryside and wildlife.

World Society for the Protection of Animals
106 Jermyn Street
London SW1Y 6EE
Works throughout the world to protect all kinds of animal life.

Worldwide Fund for Nature UK (WWF)
Panda House
Weyside Park
Godalming
Surrey GU7 1XR
Campaigns to save endangered animals worldwide.

Young Ornithologists' Club (YOC)
c/o Royal Society for the Protection of Birds (RSPB)
The Lodge
Sandy
Beds SG19 2DL
Young people's organisation that campaigns to protect birds worldwide.

Young People's Trust for the Environment and Nature Conservation
95 Woodbridge Road
Guildford
Surrey GU1 4PY
Young people's organisation that campaigns on conservation issues.

Index

Picture credits (key: l – left, r – right, t – top, c – centre, b – bottom, tl – top left, tr – top right, bl – bottom left, br – bottom right)
Ardea pages 4 (r, A. Florence; b, M. Grossnick), 8 (F. Gohier), 16–17 (t, I. Beames), 20 (b, Labat), 27 (b, J. Mason), 34 (r, H. & J. Beste), 57 (tr) & 60 (t, J.-P. Ferrero); **Auscape** page 35 (J. Foott); **Tarapada Banerjee** page 42 (r); **Bettmann Archive** page 13 (l); **British Library/India Office Library** page 32 (both); **Daan Bruysters** page 12 (b); **Bruce Coleman** pages 4 (t, E. & P. Bauer), 5 (t, J. Foott), 13 (l), 18–19 (b, P. Jackson), 23 (C. Ott), 25 (t, L. L. Rue; b, F. Greenaway), 26 (b, K. Taylor), 30–31 (M. Fogden), 34–35 (J. Foott), 41 (b, Dragesco), 42 (l, G. Cubitt), 43 (t, M. Grant), 48 (C. Zuber), 48–49 (G. Ziesler), 57 (tl, Sullivan & Rogers) & 57 (b, F. Greenaway); **CSIRO** page 27 (tl & r, P. M. Room); **R. Don** page 12 (l); **DRK Photo** page 61 (t, M. Kahl); **Ecoscene** page 62 (br, J. Wycherley); **Mark Edwards/Still Pictures** page 7 (l); **Explorer** pages 49 (t, Nadeau) & 51 (t, A. Wolf); **Greenpeace** page 49 (r); **Robert Harding** pages 18–19 (t, R. Greetham) & 51 (b, R. Cundy); **Holt Studios** page 33 (t, P. Peacock); **Hull Watch Group** page 31 (R. Wheeler-Osman); **Richard Kirby** pages 36 & 37 (t & c); **Frank Lane** pages 5 (l, W. J. Howes; c, J. Watkins), 7 (r, Silvestris), 10 (r, R. Bird), 55 (b, S. Maslowski), 59 (tr, Silvestris) & 62 (bl, L. Batten); **Trevor Lawson** page 15; **Minnesota Historical Society** page 39 (b); **Nature Conservancy Council** page 57 (c, P. Wakely); **Nature Photographers** page 44–45 (P. Sterry); **New York Zoological Society** page 45 (B. Meng); **NHPA** pages 4 (c, P. Fagot), 5 (b, M. Wendler), 21 (T. Nakamura), 29 (A. Bannister), 38 (t, Agence Nature), 47 (t, J. Shaw), 48–49 (b, J. Sauvanet), 54 (l & r, D. Woodfall), 55 (t, E. A. Janes), 56–57 (M. Leach), 60 (b, A. Bannister) & 61 (b, P. Scott); **Oxford Scientific Films** pages 22 (t, R. Jackman; bl, Animals Animals/L. L. Rue; br, F. Ehrenstrom), 30 (r, Animals Animals/J. Gerlach), 37 (b, D. Allan), 38 (bl, L. Lauber; br, S. Osolinski), 41 (r, E. Parker), 47 (b, Animals Animals/J. McDonald), 59 (br, J. Cooke) & 63 (b, C. Milkins); **Photo Researchers** page 30 (l, J. Burnley); **Planet Earth Pictures** pages 9 (P. Fioratti) & 24 (A. Shah); **Rapho** page 50–51 (H. Silvester); **RSPB** pages 10 (l, W. S. Paton) & 34 (l, R. Dennis); **Survival Anglia** pages 26–27 (N. Gordon), 33 (b, J. van Gruisen) & 53 (t, J. Mihok; b, J. Foott); **Sygma** page 14 (B. Bisson); **Arthur Tilley** page 62–63; **TSW-Click/Chicago** page 39 (t, C. Melloan); **Visum** page 20 (t, Wolfgang Steche); **Philip Wayre, Otter Trust** pages 16 (b) & 17 (both); **WWF International** page 43 (b, X. Lecoultre). The photograph on page 59 (l) was taken for the BBC by Brian Shuel.
Illustrators Graham Allen, Stephen Lings, Alan Male, Shane Marsh, Jane Pickering, Clive Pritchard, Sebastian Quigley, (Linden Artists). Richard Phipps, Helen Senior.